SUCCESS EXPRESS

HOW TO START AND PROFIT FROM YOUR OWN BUSINESS

BY DAVE DEL DOTTO

REVISED UPDATED EDITION

SUCCESS EXPRESS

HOW TO START AND PROFIT FROM YOUR OWN BUSINESS

BY DAVE DEL DOTTO

REVISED UPDATED EDITION

Copyright © 1989 by International Corporation for Financial Security, Inc.
1500 J Street • Modesto • California • 95354

TABLE OF CONTENTS

Page

ABOUT THE AUTHOR

Dave Del Dotto entered construction work after attending the University of Arizona. Eight years later, he found himself dreaming of a better life than hanging drywall for long hours, coming home exhausted, and never having the time or money to do what he really wanted for himself and his family.

In pursuit of his dreams, he sought fresh challenges and greater opportunities in real estate. He began his new career in 1979—only a few weeks before interest rates began to skyrocket toward 21 percent, and the real estate market went into a prolonged slide. Many people were unable to buy homes, and many agents and brokers went out of business.

As a new agent, Dave had an advantage over those with more experience. Before rising interest forced massive changes on the industry, everything had remained unchanged for years: low interest, and conventional lending practices. Real estate brokerages and banks were nice, conservative money trees for their owners. Those who worked in the field weren't interested in doing deals any way except the "way it's always been done."

This obsolete thinking didn't hold Dave back. Instead, he was able to analyze the problems of buying and selling in a totally changed market with a fresh and open mind. Far from being discouraged, he went to work looking for "the way it *can* be done."

He succeeded. Dave became widely known for his innovative, creative techniques.

In 1982, responding to popular demand, he wrote his first book, the classic *Creative Financing: 101 Purchase Offers Sellers Can't Resist.* He has his own TV show, has been a guest on numerous national radio and TV programs, and has given countless seminars all across the nation. He has continued to write books, and has produced a series of educational tapes, all available from the International Corporation for Financial Security, Inc.

Today, Dave lives in a million-plus dollar house on the beach in Hawaii, owns property in many states, has established the Dave Del Dotto Real Estate Executive Club for advanced investors, and is involved in a number of multi-million dollar projects.

He went for his dreams, and made them come true.

INTRODUCTION

There's a strange attitude in this country that you have to be somebody special to be an entrepreneur. Some people think you need a Master's degree from Harvard Business School, a genius I.Q., a rich family, or a streak of larceny to start and run your own business.

That's absolutely not true. Most entrepreneurs are honest people; many of them have average intelligence, while a few never got beyond the fourth grade in school; and hardly any of them come from wealthy families.

What most people do need to become entrepreneurs, however, is an introduction to some ideas they've never been exposed to before. It's not that these ideas are very difficult for the average person to grasp; they just aren't formally taught anywhere most of us are likely to come across them.

If you have an entrepreneur in your family or among your acquaintances, or if you do go to business school, you'll recognize these ideas. Unfortunately, a large number of people don't go to business school. By the time they think they should have, they believe life has already closed that choice off from them. Even more unfortunately, these are exactly the people who are least likely to know any entrepreneurs personally.

That's why I decided to write this book. I want you to understand what entrepreneurs are, how they think and what they do, and how easy it is to become one. Why should you become one? Because it's the express line to success in the United States of America. If you're interested in becoming successful — read on.

CHAPTER 1

AN OVERVIEW

W elcome to the artistic side of business.
Artistic? Certainly. Entrepreneurship is the creative, artistic side of every practical business.

To appreciate that statement, you have to understand what entrepreneurs actually do. They're the people who turn economic dreams into reality. They create the new enterprises and opportunities, mold and develop their creations into working ventures, and build those ventures into profitable businesses. Basically, an entrepreneur is someone who starts, organizes, and/or directs any undertaking. It might be a small retail store, a manufacturing company, an import business, an investment firm, a farm, or any other pursuit you can think of. In fact, technically speaking, the task the entrepreneur takes on doesn't even have to be a profit-making enterprise. It could be a charity fund drive, or a campaign to get all the neighbors on the street to plant flowers and trim their lawns.

Usually, though, when we think of entrepreneurs, we mean people who use their talents and energies to become independent businesspeople. In this book, I'm concerned with helping those men and women. Let me tell you why.

THE IMPORTANCE OF ENTREPRENEURS

The United States was the first nation founded on the idea that every citizen had the right to become whatever he wanted. It wasn't really a new idea, though. You don't need to know much history to see that the entire direction of Western civilization had been moving toward that goal for centuries, and that the movement was strongest in England. So, it was no mere chance or freak accident that the idea took root in a former English colony and, in only slightly different form, in Canada as well.

In the 18th Century "citizen" meant white males who could afford to own land. The fact that our definition is now far broader and almost all-inclusive should not blind us to the importance of this gigantic step forward.

From the beginning, we have had the right to be entrepreneurs. We didn't have to take over our father's jobs or fill positions assigned us by a king or nobleman. If we were born beggars, we didn't have to stay beggars. Our forefathers were free to try any career they wanted. If they had the ability to make a success of it, no one could step in and take the business away from them. We still have that freedom, and today it is easier than ever, and the opportunities are greater than at any time in the history of the world.

Our free business climate attracted (and still attracts) the smartest, most ambitious people from all over the globe and made us world leaders in business, industry, and invention almost before the rest of the world got around to taking our nations and our peoples seriously. It gave ordinary people the highest standard of living ever known, or even imagined.

Think of it.

Sure, royalty, political bigshots, tycoons and top athletes and entertainers all over the world (even in the Soviet Union) live better than the average American. But what about the ordinary people?

Do you have any idea how the common citizens of even many "advanced" nations live? I've done some traveling, and I can tell you that our professionals, our upper middle class, have lifestyles which match some of the richest people in many other places. Our blue-collar workers live as well or better than white collar workers in most of the rest of the world. Even those on welfare live as well as the working classes of many countries.

We regard a private home or apartment, a TV, car, and three well-balanced meals a day as basic necessities; things we take as much for granted as the air we breath. If we see a homeless person sleeping on the street, begging for food, we see it as a problem we should be solving. That person needs help. Depending on our viewpoint, we might say the person should get himself together and find a job, or the government should step in and find him a home and give him money and re-training to help him get back on his feet, or that he needs to enter a mental health care facility, or all of the above. But we *don't* regard his condition as our normal way of life.

Contrast that with Latin America. In many towns, a *Norte Americano* can't even walk around without attracting a crowd of underfed beggars. Think about India, where many millions of people beg, cook, eat, and sleep in the streets with *no* hope that anything will change, or that there is anything that they, individually, can do to better their miserable lot. Or many parts of Africa, where disease and starvation claim so many lives no one can keep accurate statistics.

I could go on, but you see the point. We are envied and imitated by the rest of the world. Even dedicated Communists wish they could live as we do. What else do you think Gorbachev's *Glasnost* and *Peristroika* mean? He and his fellow party leaders are smart enough to know that his people are tired of standing in line for hours to buy a few rolls of toilet paper; that for their people buying the basic necessities of life is an experience we encounter only when trying to buy tickets to a Bruce Springsteen concert or the last standing room tickets to the Super Bowl, and that it has to change.

Why do we have it so lucky? It isn't luck. I don't believe in luck. It is the free enterprise system, which allows us to create, buy and sell any commodity or any service for which there is a demand. (Of course, we can also do this with things for which there is no demand, but that's not an economically successful tactic. I'll tell you how to avoid this problem later on.)

ENTREPRENEURS HELP
STABILIZE OUR ECONOMY

Entrepreneurship isn't just the historical foundation of our economy, though. It's also one of the key factors that helps US survive and bounce back from worldwide economic problems more quickly than other countries can.

For instance, during the recessionary cycle that started when OPEC began raising world oil prices, most of the industrialized nations were hard hit. Many businesses cut back or closed down completely as energy prices rose, since manufacturing, heating, lighting, and shipping costs reached the point where some companies simply couldn't afford them any more. Other companies raised their prices to cover their higher costs. This made their goods or services more expensive.

As the higher prices were felt by average consumers, they decided they needed bigger paychecks to live on. Owners obliged when they could, with the result that labor costs rose. Again, some businesses raised prices to cover the increase, while others cut back the work force or closed.

When several companies close down or cut back on business at the same time, it has a domino effect on the rest of the economy. Businesses that supplied goods or services to the failing companies also lose income, since they've lost customers. Meanwhile, people who've lost their jobs have less income to spend, and are more careful about dipping into their savings or using credit. As a result, the entire economy slows down still more, so that even more businesses either cut back or fail. Everyone is caught in a downward spiral that's very difficult to stop.

That's a pretty simplified description of a fairly complicated subject, but if you plan to go into business for yourself, you have to be aware of financial cycles. Now let's see why the American system is more successful in dealing with these cycles than some other systems are. For comparison, let's look at the differences between the United States and Great Britain.

In Great Britain, people have a long tradition of looking to the upper classes to solve problems and take care of the lower classes. This goes way back to the feudal system, which if you remember your history, was based on the idea that the king and the nobility owned everything. Everyone else was a peasant, allowed to live on someone else's land, or in their house, as a reward for working the farms, building the castles, fighting in the army, or acting as a servant.

As time went on, this loosened up a little. But still, getting a new business started depended on coming up with an idea that appealed to the lord of the manor, or to the king. Then you had to get special permission from the crown to develop your idea. Without that permission, you couldn't open a shop, get a loan, or do any kind of business, unless you were literally willing to risk your neck.

Over centuries, British life discouraged individual initiative. It eventually became possible for Englishmen to become entrepreneurs, but it was difficult, and wasn't part of the background of ordinary people. Those not born to families already in business were encouraged by society to "know your place" and not try to change. In fact, many of the people who might have built the foundations of free enterprise in Great Britain ended up emigrating to America, where it was more acceptable and easier to control their own fortunes.

Then we come to the last ten years. What happened during the most recent recessionary cycle?

Thousands of Americans who lost their jobs and couldn't find another simply went out and started their own businesses. These new enterprises put money into circulation and provided more jobs for others. In some cases, the new businesses supplied jobs directly, by hiring staff; in other cases, they stimulated employment by creating more work for suppliers, which increased the suppliers' needs for labor.

Of course, this wasn't the only factor working to pull America out of recession; but it put people back to work who wouldn't have had jobs otherwise, and helped stimulate the economy.

Meanwhile, what happened in Great Britain? Thousands of people who lost their jobs in the recession simply sat and waited for someone else to put them back to work. Unfortunately, most of them are still sitting and waiting, as Britain's unemployment rate remains almost double what ours is.

As an illustration of this, my friend Bill told me about an incident in an English pub during his vacation last summer. He'd stopped in to try some of the famous British lager, and as the barmaid was serving him, a television news broadcast announced the closing of a local factory. "Oh, no!" the barmaid exclaimed. "There goes me husband's job!"

Bill expressed his sympathy, and got into conversation with the woman. It turned out that her husband had been laid off from the factory for two years, drawing unemployment — what the English call "on the dole" — simply waiting for a call to come back to work. Most of his "mates" were in the same position. Even though news from the factory was consistently poor, and it continued to lay off workers from time to time, none of these people made any effort to find anything else. They wanted to be ready when the factory called them back. And it never even occurred to them to start businesses of their own. The dole — the government — would take care of them until the factory needed them.

Contrast that with the story Sally tells of what happened when a major factory in her Midwestern American home town laid off a large number of workers. Certainly, some of the people Sally formerly worked with went on unemployment and then welfare. A few found other jobs. And others became handymen, opened tax-preparation services, got real estate licenses, or started repairing their neighbors' cars. One woman sold her baked goods to local restaurants, and a man began manufacturing wooden toys and building custom cabinets. A married couple who had both worked at the factory opened a janitorial service.

The Americans, faced with a similar situation, had a much more independent reaction than their British counterparts. It was in their American tradition of self-sufficiency and taking the initiative.

INDIVIDUAL BENEFITS OF ENTREPRENEURSHIP

Is this entrepreneurial spirit as good for the individual as it is for the country? I think so. For one thing, there's a great deal of satisfaction in being your own boss. You can never be laid off or fired.

For another thing, you know your hard work benefits you directly. You aren't working to make the boss rich, or to support an anonymous board of directors and all the stockholders.

The office or factory isn't someplace you have to put in eight hours a day, five days a week, so you can earn the right to spend a few hours a week doing what you like. When you own the business, your workplace is yours, something you can take pride in knowing you built from nothing. If it weren't for you, that business wouldn't exist.

No one else can assign you distasteful tasks and demand you do them to someone else's standards, or on someone else's schedule. You decide what jobs you'll do, on what schedule, and how well they have to be done. The things you hate to do, or are simply no good at, you delegate to someone else. And you tell the others when the work has to be done.

Besides all this, though — security, self-determination, pride, and authority — entrepreneurship offers one more satisfaction you rarely find in any other job. It offers you the opportunity to become wealthy.

You don't get rich working for others. You get a salary, paid vacations, and a small pension. The person who owns the company you work for gets the mansion, the yacht, the Mercedes, the diamonds and furs, extended trips to Hawaii, Europe, and the Orient, and early retirement to a tropical paradise.

Which would you rather be: the loyal employee who scrapes along from paycheck to paycheck for forty years, only to spend retirement trying to figure out how to pay for food, heat, rent, and medical care with an inadequate Social Security check — or wealthy enough to retire while you're still young enough to enjoy everything your fortune can pay for?

I know which choice is mine. I made it years ago, and now I'm enjoying the benefits.

Many people won't make the same choice I did. They're afraid of the risks; or they don't like responsibility; or they don't want to work as hard as they're afraid they'd have to for success. That's their choice, and I have to respect it. After all, those people make it possible for entrepreneurs like me to expand our companies and go from simply prosperous to truly wealthy. We hire them to do all the work we don't want to, or don't have time for. Once our companies get large enough, they do all the work — and we keep the profits their work brings in.

Is that unfair to the workers? I don't think so. They have the same opportunities I had, or any other entrepreneur has, to become an owner instead of a worker. Starting a business, building it into a successful company, managing it for larger profits, expanding it, and setting up systems so that the enterprise will continue running profitably does involve risk and hard work. The profits from that business are the entrepreneur's reward for taking the risk, putting in the work, and at the same time providing jobs for others and contributing to our nation's wealth.

Obviously, though, you're interested in earning the rewards of business ownership, or you wouldn't be reading this book. You realize that if you must work a certain number of hours in your life, it's far more satisfying, both personally and financially, to work for yourself rather than someone else. You want to know what it takes to become an entrepreneur — and I want to tell you. Is that possible, though?

ARE ENTREPRENEURS A DIFFERENT BREED?

Some people believe entrepreneurs are born, not made. We all knew some child, when we were growing up, who always had a money-making scheme going. He was the first one to open a lemonade stand — next to the lot where the rest of the kids played ball. He ran errands, mowed lawns, did other people's homework, sold frogs that cost him nothing to catch, fixed bikes, painted cars, and generally hustled to make a buck. Maybe today he owns an auto dealership or his own computer company.

That kid had something special going for him, all right. Maybe he was just born wanting independence and money more than the rest of us did. Or perhaps he had a relative or adult friend who encouraged him and helped him come up with ideas. What's most likely, though, is that he needed more money than his family could or would give him in the form of allowances and gifts. Since job opportunities for children are limited, he formed the habit of looking for ways to make a profit and then putting those ideas into action.

Many of our most successful entrepreneurs come from very poor families. Simple survival is their motivation for wanting to earn money when they're young. As they grow older, their early experience helps them build adult success.

Other successful people come from backgrounds where they had enough to live on, but not enough for something extra that was very important to them. Many people tell me they first started trying to earn money as children because their families couldn't afford things the child wanted a great deal — movies every Saturday, dancing lessons, a new bicycle, a second car, better clothes, etc.

Cases like these sound as though they support the idea that successful entrepreneurs start young. Actually, though, they illustrate a different point quite as well. They show that when the desire is strong enough, even a child can learn to be an entrepreneur.

An entrepreneur is simply someone who has learned to behave in certain ways. The entrepreneur develops habits and ways of working that support independent success. These characteristics have been observed by researchers and students, and can be taught. You can learn them.

I've done it myself, and I've seen my students do it. You don't have to take my word for it, though. Courses in how to become an entrepreneur are now taught at some of our leading universities. Students of these courses have learned to change their outlook and behaviors so that instead of training to be lifelong employees, they're now embarking on careers as business founders and owners.

Naturally, you can't expect to become a successful entrepreneur overnight. And no one can guarantee that your first effort, or even your twenty-first, will be successful. There are dozens of variables involved in establishing a successful enterprise, from choosing the right business and location to hiring the best people to work for you. Besides that, there are hundreds of factors, some under your control and many beyond it, that can affect your success. These can range from your own health and your family's support to world economic trends, government policies, and new inventions.

With so many influences on the stability of any business, it's impossible for me to present you with a detailed blueprint and say,

"If you do exactly what I tell you, within two years you'll own a successful business that will support you in luxury the rest of your life and allow you to retire in five years."

I'd like to say that just as much as you'd probably like to hear it. The fact is, though, no one's ever found such a formula. Or if they have, they're keeping it secret. The truth is, starting and running a business always involves the risk of failure. The true secret to success is not to let that stop you.

Somewhere along the line, you've probably seen the list of Abraham Lincoln's accomplishments. Between 1832 and 1860 he lost jobs, was defeated in elections and turned down for appointive offices, his sweetheart died, and he had a complete nervous breakdown. Yet he never gave up trying, and eventually he was elected president.

Or how about Thomas Edison searching for the filament that would make the electric lightbulb succeed? After trying a thousand different materials, he said he now knew "one thousand things that didn't work." Every time we turn on a lamp or drive down a city street at night, we see the proof that Edison didn't give up.

THE TRUE SECRET OF SUCCESS

Right there is the basic key to success in business, or in anything else, for that matter. Whether you call it tenacity, stick-to-it-iveness, stubbornness, or guts, successful entrepreneurs are those who keep trying. If one approach doesn't solve a problem, they look for a different approach or redefine the problem. When one effort fails, they look for a new opportunity where they can apply the lessons they learned on their previous try. After the Ford Motor Company came out with the Edsel, they didn't stop making cars simply because that particular model was the biggest failure in the history of auto design.

Persistence is the trait that pays off time after time. Track coach Bill Bowerman couldn't get anyone interested in the shoe he designed for his student runners in the mid-1950s. When the big sporting goods companies turned down his design, Bowerman didn't throw his plans in a drawer and forget about them. Instead, he was stubborn enough to make the shoes himself, by hand, so that at least the athletes who trained under him would have the kind of shoes he thought they needed. Finally, in 1962, one of those runners was in a position to form a company with his former coach. Today their Nike Inc. brings in over one billion dollars a year in sales.

FINDING THE PERFECT OPPORTUNITY

Politics, lightbulbs, autos, running shoes — four very different areas where people tried, failed, and later succeeded. There are as many different business possibilities as there are people to put them into action. Do you see why it's so difficult to tell you one magical system to follow? Every individual is different, with his or her own goals, desires, background, and personal situation. Every town, every state, every section of the country has its own resources, opportunities, and potential drawbacks. Laws and customs differ, and the world changes every day.

No, I can't give you the failsafe blueprint that works for everyone. What I can give you, though, is the guidelines you can use to develop your own personal, individualized plan. Once you know the general rules and principles to follow, you can use them to design the one career that's best for you.

Personally, I think that's better. The business that works for me may not be right for you. Besides, our economy isn't static. Laws change, prices go up and down, fashions and fads come and go. Today's best business opportunity can become tomorrow's one-way ticket to disaster. If all of us only know one system to follow to success in one particular enterprise, we're all in trouble if that industry hits hard times.

But if we know the general guidelines we can apply to any form of business, anywhere, and how to tailor those guidelines to individual situations, we have the flexibility to respond to anything that happens. We can change our business, move into another geographical area, or go into a different business completely if changing times or our own interests indicate these are good moves for us.

Of course, you have to realize that starting and running any business is really too large a subject to cover in this one small manual. If you look in the business section of your local library, you'll find shelves and shelves of books on general practices, as well as specialized books for particular industries. Colleges often have entire libraries devoted to business subjects alone.

Many of these books, though, are overly technical and downright intimidating. Sometimes I think the main object of a lot of the authors is to discourage the average person into thinking business is too complicated for us ordinary folks. Maybe they think we should leave it to the Ph.D.s. Only they're all so busy writing books, teaching classes, and arguing over their theories and formulas that they don't have time to bother with the daily details of attending to business. So what would happen to our economy if we left it to them?

What I want to do with this manual is show beginners how to become successful entrepreneurs. You won't need a college education or special tutoring in mathematical analysis to understand the concepts I'll show you. And we won't get involved in a lot of theoretical technicalities that only matter to the college professors. I'll show you how real people make real money by starting and running real enterprises in the United States and Canada today.

And since I can't cover everything in this one book, and I can't tell you exactly what you should do in every possible situation that applies to your individual ambition, I'll suggest some other resources for you. You'll need particular kinds of information in specialty areas, and advice that applies to your business in your town. I'll recommend resources for you.

When you've finished this book, you won't know everything you've always wanted to know about how to operate an Armenian restaurant in Bismarck, North Dakota, or a gadget factory in Little Rock, Arkansas. What you will know is how to get started in any business that interests you, and where to go to learn more about the particular business you want.

Learning, after all, is a lifelong journey. And so is success. Every journey starts somewhere; it's my hope that this manual can be your first step in reaching your goal of successful entrepreneurship.

CHAPTER 2

HOW DO
ENTREPRENEURS
WORK?

I mentioned in the introductory chapter that all entrepreneurs aren't born with the characteristics for success. Through my own life and observations, and in reading books by others who study success, I've come up with a list of a dozen traits common to entrepreneurs.

Keep in mind that these traits aren't born into any of us. They're trained in, whether early in life, when we aren't even aware of the process, or later, when we consciously try to acquire them. It's not true that your personality and behaviors are permanently one way or another from birth. Most of our actions, reactions, and even ways of thinking are taught to us. That's why humans can change in response to their environments.

Therefore, most of these success traits are available to all of us. If some of them seem foreign to your personality, it's because you aren't used to using them. It takes only thirty days of daily practice to form a new habit, so if you worked on acquiring one of these traits for a month, and then went on to the next and spent a month on that one, and so on, at the end of a year, you'd have them all.

Also, as in anything, most of these characteristics can turn into drawbacks if carried to extremes. As we go through and discuss each one, I'll try to point out the problems in carrying them too far.

1. MOTIVATED

Entrepreneurs usually are strongly motivated to be their own bosses. In fact, most of them can't stand working for others. They don't like to take orders, and they want to do everything their own way, on their own schedule. Some of these people can even be a real problem in a team working situation. They often question procedures, argue with authority, and complain until they destroy the morale of those around them.

You don't have to carry it this far. But if you don't feel you have enough motivation to run a business, start asking yourself questions about your job. Can you see ways to improve a product or procedure? How would you handle the company if you were in charge? Once you start thinking like this on a regular basis, it can build into a powerful desire to do things your own way.

Another prime motivator for entrepreneurs is money. The largest rewards in business go to those who take the risks. If your salary is never going to be enough, you can only hope to increase your income to the level you really want through business ownership.

Remember, however, that there are no guarantees, and the big money doesn't always come early to entrepreneurs. You may have to make several starts before you hit on an idea that works. After that, profits may have to go back into the business to build it for several years before you can afford to pay yourself what you feel you deserve. If you're patient and willing to work for it, though, the proceeds from owning a business can be far greater than any salary you could hope to earn working for someone else.

Finally, power is a strong motivation for some entrepreneurs.

It's not the kind of thing many people talk about openly, but if you can get them to speak honestly, a lot of successful people will admit that power is a very pleasant thing to have. Of course, if you abuse your power and become a tyrant, you can spoil your own success. Good people won't stay with you if you treat them like slaves, and potential clients will avoid you.

Used carefully, power can make life more pleasant for you and those around you. Powerful people make things happen, and other people seek them out. That's not a bad motivation, even if you don't admit it to others.

2. ACTION ORIENTED

Entrepreneurs don't sit around talking about their big ideas, or what they're going to do when they get the chance. When they have an idea, they go into action. They understand that if they want to reach their goals, they must take the initiative.

This doesn't mean entrepreneurs run off in all directions trying to do things before they've researched the possibilities. Their actions include thoughtful assessment of opportunities and alternatives. But research is action, too. Rather than sit around daydreaming about how to spend all the money a new idea could bring in, an entrepreneur gets busy on the necessary steps to make the idea a working reality.

Beginnings aren't the only places where entrepreneurs act, either. They keep going, one task after another, until all the pieces fall into place. They don't procrastinate, or waste time on activities that don't contribute to their goals. They may work on one goal at a time, or spend time on more than one project during a day, but they spend all their working hours in productive efforts.

A certain amount of daydreaming is necessary, of course, to generate the ideas the entrepreneur will act on. But once those ideas come, the successful person doesn't put off mundane tasks involved in laying the groundwork to make something happen.

3. Healthy

Health is a relative term, of course. I've known handicapped people who run businesses, and people with serious physical problems who reach their goals. But successful entrepreneurs understand that they must keep themselves in the best possible state of health for their own condition. When you're in charge of your future, any day you spend lying in bed or sitting in a doctor's office is more than a day lost in reaching your goal. You can miss important appointments, lose out on a profitable opportunity, or alienate a potentially good customer if you're out of action at the crucial time.

It takes energy to direct a business, especially in the start-up phases, so you want to be sure all the strength you're capable of is available to use. That means both physically and mentally.

Don't fall into the trap that hurts so many ambitious people. It often seems there are so many tasks to do, jobs that must be handled personally by the entrepreneur, that he or she spends every waking hour working on the business. Meals are skipped, sleep is lost, and exercise and recreation become fading memories.

This may be all right for short spurts, or while particular problems are being solved, but don't let it become a way of life. If you don't have a regular diet and exercise regime, now is the time to start. See your doctor for a complete physical and recommendations for a fitness program that's right for you. Then watch your diet, get a full night's sleep every night, and set aside time every single day to exercise.

Keep mentally fit by making time for relaxation and some of your favorite activities. Get completely away from work and forget about it entirely from time to time. When you do, you'll find you come back refreshed, with new energy to tackle your work and a fresh perspective on any problems you're facing.

Many busy executives recommend mini-vacations. They leave home for a weekend alone, or with their families or other favorite people, and spend two or three days relaxing at something completely removed from business. Some say when they do this at least once a month, they really don't feel the need for a long vacation every year.

4. INDEPENDENT

When you first go into business, you may have to be prepared to do everything yourself. You might not start with a secretary, an executive assistant, or a group of people who tidy up your projects and make them presentable after you've been messily creative.

Eventually, of course, your goal is to be able to hire all the help you need. But in the beginning you may be all alone. People who are used to working in managerial jobs sometimes forget how much they rely on a support staff. Sending out letters, answering incoming mail, making copies, filing, doing the accounts, filling out government forms, and answering the telephone are as important as meeting with new clients and attracting investors. Also, the more informed you are about the basic running of your enterprise, the better you'll be able to judge when your future employees are performing well and when they aren't.

5. FLEXIBLE

As I mentioned in the previous chapter, our economy changes. This means business must change with it, to take advantage of new opportunities and discard outmoded practices.

Naturally, business doesn't change by itself. People make the changes, and an astute entrepreneur has to be ready to either redesign an existing business, or to start a new one, as necessary.

In addition, a business owner has to stay flexible enough to take in new information and make decisions. There are rarely any cut-and-dried, one-size-fits-all standard solutions in any situation. It's up to you, as an entrepreneur, to sift through whatever information is available to you and then choose the course of action that seems most reasonable to you on the basis of what you know and believe.

This is one of the greatest freedoms of being your own boss, but for some people it's uncomfortable. They want to go through life knowing what's going to happen next and believing that somewhere the perfect answer exists for every question.

Actually, life isn't really like that at all, for anyone anywhere. Every moment we're on this earth, we run the chance of getting into an unexpected situation and having to improvise our way out of it. True security lies in knowing you can cope with whatever comes your way. And the only method there is for giving yourself that security is practice. As the German philosopher Nietzsche said, "That which does not kill me makes me stronger."

Experienced entrepreneurs know this. After several years of steering their own course, they've lived through failures and recovered from them to go on to greater victories. They know that come bad times or good, they'll always find a way to survive, and that the more adversity they survive, the more they learn to help them prosper in their next effort. Most of all, they know an important part of success is flexibility, the ability to accept and adapt to new situations.

6. DETERMINED

Entrepreneurs don't give up easily. When they're successful, this is called "perseverance"; before they succeed, or if they fail, it's called "stubborn," "bullheaded," "arrogant," or "foolish."

Well, maybe you need to be all of these to succeed in business. There are certainly enough sensible people in the world who give up when their wise friends and relatives tell them their ideas are sure to fail. We call them "employees."

Seriously, it does take determination to be an entrepreneur. You have to make up your mind that you'll reach your goal no matter what problems come up along the way. Otherwise, the first time you face a problem you hadn't anticipated, you're likely to abandon your efforts instead of looking for a solution.

Yes, determination can be carried too far. I've seen people hanging on to businesses long past the time when they should have realized nothing will save them. It's not always easy to let go of something you've put all your time and effort and pride into during years of your life.

How do you know when this is the case? I'd say if you're working harder than you ever have and bringing in less and less money; if you keep running into the same problems or making the same mistakes over and over; and if you can't sleep or relax or enjoy life any more, it's time to think long and hard about getting out of that business.

Don't act too hastily, though. First, call in a consultant or two. Perhaps they can suggest some changes you hadn't thought of. Sit down with your key workers and ask their opinions. Have an accountant review your books carefully and look for ways to cut expenses and improve profits. Sometimes a business has to go through a painful readjustment just before it becomes the most profitable — and if you weren't determined, you'd give up too soon.

7. DECISIVE

Obviously, as an entrepreneur, you have to make decisions. When you're in charge, no one else will tell you what to do.

In addition, you have to make decisions firmly, often in a short time and with inadequate information. We all face this from time to time, whether we own businesses or not. The best tactic for doing this is simply to make the best decision you can based on the facts available, and then be ready to modify your choice when you know more about the situation. But don't worry about it, and don't second-guess yourself.

What I mean by that is, don't make a decision, go home and worry all night about whether it was right, then go in the next day and tell everyone to do the direct opposite of what you said the day before. If you dig up new information, or receive proof you were completely wrong, then you can change direction.

When you run a business, as much as eighty percent of your time may be devoted to solving problems. You have to be able to decide what's right in each situation and then go on to the next one. If you spend much time agonizing over whether you made the right choice on all your previous decisions, you'll soon carry around a load of doubt and worry that will make it impossible to function. You'll put so much energy into rerunning the past that you won't be able to deal with the present or plan for the future.

Another important part of decision-making is knowing when to decide right away, and when to put off a final decision. In general, small decisions can usually be made quickly, or can be delegated to almost any employee. On the other hand, you have to recognize when a choice is more important and should be investigated further.

A good rule of thumb is: Allocate your time according to how much the decision will affect costs. When it's a low-cost decision, get it out of the way as quickly as possible. When large sums of money are involved, spend as much time as you can getting all the information possible.

One special note is in order here. Some people use the same guideline in hiring staff. They figure a minimum-wage file clerk doesn't have to be screened as carefully as a high-salaried executive. Up to a point, this is true. But only up to a point. The most insignificant employees can have a big impact on your profits if they steal, disrupt the office, or use their jobs to spy for your competition. Establish minimum standards for hiring, and always check backgrounds and references. We'll go into this more fully in the chapter on assembling your team.

8. SELF-SUFFICIENT

This may sound the same as the characteristic I labeled "independent," but it's not. When I spoke of independence, I talked about being able to do everything necessary to get your business off the ground before you can afford to hire all the backup staff most large companies supply.

When I speak of self-sufficiency, I mean the trait of taking responsibility for yourself and your work. Every successful entrepreneur is very aware that to win, you must be the one who makes everything happen. No one else is going to go out there and do it for you. You have to take care of yourself and your business. What your company does or doesn't do is your direct responsibility.

This takes a lot of self-discipline. There will be jobs you hate doing, and days when you don't feel like doing anything. Later, when you can hire a small staff, you still have to show responsibility. If you shove all the dirty jobs off on your employees while you rake off the gravy, you'll encourage dissatisfaction and goofing off.

You can think what you want about the sorry state of American labor, but the truth is, your staff is only human. How would you feel in their place? You're responsible for seeing the work is done, and done right. As long as you're in charge — you must be in charge. You can't afford to indulge yourself until your business reaches the point where you can function as an absentee owner.

When you can hire top managerial talent to come in and take over the day-to-day running of your business, only consulting you occasionally for advice on where you want the company to go next — that's when you can sleep in, take long vacations, and generally pamper yourself. Even then, though, you must be available to at least one key person who can be trusted to contact you only when your input is really needed.

9. CONVINCING

You must be able to convince people to go along with you if you want to succeed as an entrepreneur. You'll have to convince people to invest in your ideas, to give you good terms on contracts, to work for you, to spend money on your product.

The most important quality you can have is sincerity. If you really believe in your idea or product, this belief will be one of the most persuasive tools at your disposal.

If you don't believe in what you're offering — why are you doing it? To be successful as an entrepreneur, you have to be enthusiastic about your own business. You must feel you're offering something that's unique, or the best available. This is no time to be humble or to indulge in false modesty. If you've invested your time, your energy, your own money in this project, you must believe people will pay for its benefits. Let that belief come through in your words and voice every time you talk about your company.

The second most important quality you need to be convincing is the ability to communicate. If you can't put your plans into words that appeal to those you deal with, they'll never know what a great opportunity you're offering them.

Convincing people is a matter of salesmanship and negotiating skills. You may think you aren't a "born salesman." Don't let that stop you. The more intelligent and sophisticated people are, the more they're turned off by someone they believe is trying to pull a sales job on them. And intelligent, sophisticated people are the ones most likely to have money to invest or spend with your company.

To learn how to communicate with others, take a public speaking course. These are offered at community colleges, by adult education programs, and through an organization called Toastmasters that's active in most cities across the country. Or take a job, either full- or part-time, that offers sales training.

I know this may sound like I'm asking the impossible from some of you. I can't count the number of people I've talked to who thought speaking in front of strangers would literally kill them. But the fact is, it won't.

Ask yourself, "What's the worst thing that can happen if I talk to these people? Will they throw tomatoes and hiss? Will they put me in jail, take away my children, beat me to a pulp, let the air out of my tires?"

Taking it to extremes shows you how unnecessary your fears are. Then imagine your entire audience, whether it's one person or a roomful, sitting there in their underwear. Pretend they're doing something human but undignified, such as picking their noses or cutting their toenails. Why should you be afraid of folks who act like that?

Force yourself to speak up, and you'll be thankful the rest of your life, whether you end up owning a multinational corporation or just want to make new friends at a neighborhood barbecue.

10. CONFIDENT

If you're going to succeed as an entrepreneur, you must have confidence — in yourself, in your abilities, and in your business.

You can't step away from your average family, friends, or acquaintances and start doing business for yourself without confidence. You must believe you have the qualities to make something more of yourself, and that your business deserves to earn recognition and money.

You have to like yourself enough to feel you deserve the best life has to offer. You must be confident in your ability to find and develop a business opportunity that will benefit its customers and enrich you, its founder.

However, you don't want to build this feeling to the point where you believe you're infallible. No one is perfect. Success is not synonymous with godhood. When you start thinking no one can tell you anything, you're over-compensating for hidden fears of inferiority.

The truly confident person listens to other points of view with an open mind. If someone else's ideas or opinions make sense, the confident person can adopt them and blend them into an overall plan. Confidence combined with an open mind and the ability to make decisions is an unbeatable business attribute.

11. THRIFTY

An entrepreneur must watch the bottom line at all times. But you'll notice I recommend you be thrifty, not miserly. Reasonable expenditures for items that help your business grow and prosper must be made.

You have to learn the value of money and the proper places to spend it or cut corners. For instance, sometimes you can save by buying secondhand equipment and furniture. But don't buy something old and beat up if repairs and lost work time will wipe out your savings.

I've seen many business owners try to save money by furnishing offices or factories with equipment so old that it breaks down frequently. As a result, workers spend time trying to do minor repairs themselves. When they're unsuccessful, they stand idly by waiting for repairmen to get the equipment running again. Meanwhile, schedules are delayed, and rush jobs have to be farmed out to other sources. The final outcome? Missed deadlines, high costs for repair bills and outside suppliers, employees paid for unproductive hours, and lowered morale among workers frustrated by their substandard equipment. And that doesn't even consider the cost of lost clients or customers who may take their business elsewhere when schedules aren't met or their jobs aren't done as well as they could be.

Certainly you should try to get the most you can for your money. But learn the difference between real savings and false economy. The place to hold down costs without damaging your capacity to do business is on the frills.

Luxury offices with thick pile carpet, original artwork, designer furniture, and an impressive reception lounge are nice, but are they necessary? As the owner, you may feel you're entitled to an executive suite, a fancy conference room, an impressive home, and an expensive new car every year. But can the business honestly support it?

Yes, the rewards of the business are yours, and you deserve them as soon as the business can provide them. However, this is an area where you must exercise honesty and self-discipline with yourself. Many, many businesses fail when the entrepreneur takes out too much too soon.

For the first few years the needs of your office, factory, or shop must come first. Later on you'll have plenty of time to enjoy a fancy lifestyle. And you'll enjoy it more, and for a longer time, if you wait until the business is financially secure. If you don't wait, and start squandering money that should go back into building up your enterprise, you could easily lose everything you've worked for.

12. Informed

To be successful, an entrepreneur has to know what's going on in the world, especially as it affects his or her business. What's selling, what isn't, who's buying, and how much they're willing to pay are all facts you must know to survive in the marketplace.

In addition, you have to pay attention to future trends and possibilities that might influence your costs, profits, or product. Where does your product or raw material come from? What's the political situation there? How reliable is transportation? Would a trade embargo or revolution in South Africa cut you off from an important supplier? Would higher wage agreements in Taiwan increase your costs? Are there other places you could go for comparable goods at reasonable prices? If not, what else might your company make or sell instead? How difficult would it be to change directions?

The entrepreneur also needs to keep track of lifestyle trends in the market population. In the United States, this might mean being aware that aging Baby Boomers increase the market for products that appeal to people in their forties and fifties.

Geographical population shifts often indicate market shifts. For example, the large numbers of people moving out of the northern states and into the sunbelt mean smaller sales for winter clothing, but increased demand for lighter wear.

If you're interested in this market, take a closer look at who actually is moving. Older folks retiring to Florida might want loose shifts and sports shirts, while young professionals heading for Atlanta need lightweight business clothes and sexy sportswear.

To get information like this, you'll need to subscribe to the leading trade journal for your industry and keep an eye on national and world news. If you depend heavily on another business, you should subscribe to the trade journal for that industry also. For example, if you manufacture plastic widgets, you should take a plastics journal as well as Widget Weekly. And if you ship your widgets by train, you'd better keep track of what the railroads are up to as well.

There you have my twelve positive entrepreneurial characteristics. To recap, I've listed them in the chart on the next page. How many of them do you have? Which ones would you like to acquire?

Don't give up already if you don't fit this profile at all. As I said at the beginning of this chapter, every one of these traits can be learned. All it takes is a conscious shift in some of your learned attitudes and behaviors.

TWELVE TRAITS OF SUCCESSFUL ENTREPRENEURS

1. Motivated — Want to reach your goal more than anything else

2. Action oriented — Invest time in working toward your goal, not in daydreaming or useless activities

3. Healthy — Keep yourself in your best possible physical and mental condition

4. Independent — Able to work alone, if necessary, on every task toward your goal

5. Flexible — Accept and adapt to changing conditions

6. Determined — Don't give up on a good idea because of temporary problems or lack of faith from others

7. Decisive — Make the best choice available with the information you have, then go on to the next task

8. Self-sufficient — Realize you are responsible for every step of your success

9. Convincing — Use your belief and enthusiasm to persuade others

10. Confident — Believe in yourself and your ideas

11. Thrifty — Spend money only where necessary for the success of your enterprise until profits can support frills

12. Informed — Know what's going on and how it affects your business

You may doubt this. But psychologists have known for almost a century that most of our attitudes and actions are the result of habit. Habits are learned, and habits can be changed.

If you want to change a habit, you first have to become aware of it. Next, decide what new behavior you want to put in place of the old one. Then, every time you find yourself following your old pattern, make the conscious choice to substitute the new behavior you've chosen in place of the old one.

For instance, say you've decided to work on your confidence. There are many good books and tapes available on developing self-confidence and assertive behavior. Study them and decide which areas you need to work on to feel and look more confident. Let's say for example that you realize you believe others usually know more and have better ideas than you. This attitude is so habitual that you defer to others even when you're actually sure you have a better idea.

Once you're aware of this, you'll start noticing times you keep quiet rather than risk arguing when someone else makes a decision you believe is wrong. Your next step is to speak up. Give the reasons you believe some other course of action would be better.

It may take a few tries before you learn to present your reasons clearly and forcefully enough to persuade others your ideas are better. But you'll find interesting changes taking place both inside and outside yourself just from making those first efforts.

When you present your point of view, you'll begin feeling better about yourself simply because you have spoken up. That's a step in building your confidence. At the same time, others will start looking at you with new respect. Instead of seeing you as dull old George or Georgia who always goes along with the majority, they'll begin to realize you have a mind of your own.

As you gain experience and learn to present your views persuasively, sometimes you'll convince others to go along with you. Your success will increase your confidence again. And as you become known as a person with good, interesting ideas, others will start asking your opinion. Again, this new consideration for you will increase your confidence.

This process of change, whether it's for increased confidence or any other new habit you want, won't take place overnight. There's a gradual progression recognized by people who study behavioral changes. It's a four-step process that's been broken down this way:

1. Look what I did. (Recognition of a behavior you want to change.)

2. I did it again. (Realization that this behavior is a habit you're

going to have to guard against.)

3. I almost did it again. (Noticing you're about to fall into your old habit before you actually do it; this gives you the opportunity to substitute the new behavior you prefer.)

4. I don't do that any more. (The point where you've successfully broken your old habit.)

Some people say they can't change. What they really mean is, they won't. Their old way of doing things is comfortable — not because it's so rewarding, but simply because that's the way they're used to acting.

Yes, change can be uncomfortable. It can be a little frightening to try new things, especially if you're afraid it might turn you into a new, strange, different person. But changing the ways you're used to thinking and acting doesn't mean you can't change back.

If you really don't like feeling confident, staying healthy, being independent, or any of the other success traits, give them up. It's easy to slide back into habits we learned when we were young.

But if you truly want to be successful, at least try to change characteristics that can hold you back. Although it feels strange at first, you'll soon get used to being active, motivated, and determined. You might even find you'll enjoy it more than the way you were before. Why not give yourself the chance to be the best, most successful you possible?

While we're on the subject of being your best, I'd like to discuss the business field that gives you the best opportunity for fulfilling your entrepreneurial dreams. That's such a big subject, though, that we're going to take the entire next chapter to look into it.

CHAPTER 3

CHOOSING YOUR BEST OPPORTUNITY

You may already know exactly what business you want to go into — or at least you think you do. Even so, I'd advise you to pay close attention to the information we're going to cover in this chapter. If you've thought your ambition through carefully, this will serve to reinforce your confidence in your plan.

If, however, you've overlooked some key point in making your decision, this discussion could bring it to your attention. And if you aren't sure what field to concentrate on, we should be able to at least narrow down the possibilities.

As I said in Chapter One, I can't tell you what business you should enter. Personally, I happen to think real estate investment is the one best place anyone in America can make large amounts of money quickly and easily. Also, buying low-cost merchandise at auctions and reselling it is a great way to accumulate ready cash.

However, those are my choices. They may not suit you. Or you may have used those avenues to raise the money you need to start another business. And it's always possible that you simply want a change in your life and are looking for a new field with fresh challenges.

EXPLOIT YOUR STRENGTHS

The first thing you need to do, whatever your reasons for looking into new business ventures, is assess your strengths and weaknesses. Go back to Chapter Two and review the Twelve Traits of Successful Entrepreneurs. Which of these traits do you already possess? Write them here.

Now, which traits do you think you could acquire within a short time? List them here.

Finally, which of the twelve success traits do you feel would be most difficult to acquire and would take you a long time to develop? Write those here.

This gives you an overview of your strong and weak points. There's no crime in not having every success characteristic. You can run into problems, though, if you don't know your strengths and weaknesses.

Once you're aware of these traits in yourself, you can concentrate on businesses where you can make the most of your strengths, and where your weaknesses have the least influence. In addition, you can also consider looking for partners, or hiring assistants, whose abilities and shortcomings balance your own.

For instance, if you're strong on motivation and action, but have trouble being flexible or thrifty, you might look for a partner who's just the opposite. Let your partner watch the cash flow and suggest when the business should change directions, while you supply the energy to keep the company moving. If you're confident and like to stay informed, but can't face all the detail work involved in being totally independent, find someone who likes organizing an enterprise. At the very least, remind yourself to be especially careful about areas where your weak points might cause problems.

LEARN WHAT YOU LIKE

Next, what kind of work really interests you? Are you fascinated with manufacturing processes or construction? Do you like sales? Would you like to own a retail outlet? Can you see yourself supplying specialized services? Is there a field of art or creative production you'd like to be associated with?

If you're not too sure of your preferences, do some research. Find out what types of businesses exist, and which offer good opportunities. (Your local library and bookstores will be helpful here.) Check into some of the magazines now published especially for entrepreneurs, such as *Success!* and *Venture*. Also, talk to people who are active in your local Chamber of Commerce, city or county planning commission, or community redevelopment agency. They can often suggest enterprises needed in your area, and may even be able to help you get financing or grants.

As you become familiar with the variety of businesses possible to you, some will appeal to you more than others. Write down what these are, and list the reasons you like them. This will help you see the pattern to your preferences and what's important to you in a career.

While you're defining your business interests, there are some facts you should be aware of. First of all, the most difficult fields to break into are the overcrowded ones. There is more competition, and less opportunity, making it difficult to launch a successful new enterprise and keep it running profitably in these areas.

AVOID CROWDS

What are the most overcrowded fields? Traditionally, the ones everyone wants to get into: the so-called "glamor" businesses; "fun" businesses that look easy to start and seem to earn a lot of money for very little effort; popular hobbies turned into moneymaking enterprises; and the businesses "everybody knows" are hot.

You probably know by now that becoming a successful seminar speaker, writer, entertainer, or artist is much more difficult than it looks from the outside. You may not have considered, though, that catering, flower shops and nurseries, interior decorating, and public relations are difficult fields to get into.

A few people can make money from their crafts and hobbies, but it takes extra determination, motivation, and long hard hours in addition to talent and a touch of luck. (Also, some people who turn their hobbies into a job complain that they no longer enjoy macrame, woodworking, ceramics, or whatever when they have to meet production schedules and quotas. Think about that before you turn an enjoyable leisure pursuit into a career.)

And as for "hot opportunities" — well, by the time everybody knows how hot they are, the field is usually already overcrowded. If you have inside information that enables you to get your business running before everyone else realizes the profit potential, you stand the best chance of success. But remember the video game arcade fad of the early 1980s. For a while there, it seemed like a new arcade opened every week. They sprang up all over cities, and even most small towns usually had one or two. Then practically overnight the customers disappeared and arcades went out of business faster than they opened. Towns that once supported five game parlors now have one, or none.

In addition to these highly competitive fields, there's one other occupation I advise people to avoid if they possibly can — restaurants.

Every good cook who enjoys puttering in the kitchen seems to dream of owning a restaurant. Friends and family can be most encouraging about this, even those who are usually negative about other business ventures. Maybe they're thinking of the free meals they'll enjoy, and the prestige of introducing their friends to the owner.

Most of these dreamers don't seem to understand that a restaurant is a highly organized, extremely competitive business. Cooking has very little to do with the ultimate success of the venture; in fact, judging by some places I've eaten, cooking may not matter at all. Location, decoration, atmosphere, hiring and managing good help, advertising, and getting the right publicity, however, are vital to restaurant success. If you can combine these factors with good food, then you stand a reasonable chance of succeeding.

I realize, of course, that some of you won't be discouraged by my advice. If you're determined to open an art gallery, start a restaurant, or cash in on the newest fad, you'll do it in spite of me. And with that kind of determination, you may make a success of it. But before you go ahead, be sure you do the rest of your groundwork as thoroughly as possible.

You may wonder why I've spent so much time in this chapter telling you a lot of things I don't recommend. If I didn't know myself better, I'd say I've said some things that are downright discouraging.

Let me explain by telling you about the time I visited a friend of mine who's an actor in Hollywood. You'd never have heard of him. He isn't a handsome leading man or an action-adventure hero, and he doesn't get top billing. He makes a few commercials, gets an occasional bit part in a movie or television show, and acts and directs in small local theatres.

My friend, Mike, had just been asked to speak to his daughter's high school drama class on acting as a profession. I wondered what he planned to say, and he told me, "The main thing I want to tell them is that acting is the hardest career to get into in the world. And once they're in, the hours are long, the working conditions impossible, and many of the people they'll be working with are the most unpleasant you'll ever meet. I'm going to say that if they have any other talent, any other job they can do, they should choose that over acting."

That seemed pretty harsh advice to me, and I said so. After all, wasn't it possible that some really talented youngsters would be turned off by this bleak view and never give acting a try?

"If they can be turned off by what I say, they should be," Mike replied. "People who give up that easily aren't cut out for this business. They'd never be able to stick with it long enough to be successful. And the ones who will become successful are going to act no matter what I or anybody else says."

In a way, that's what I'm trying to do for you with my negative views on some of the most popular business ventures. These enterprises can be very successful for those who are totally dedicated and love what they're doing more than anything in the world. Even if the business should fail, these people will be happy that at least they got to try what they always dreamed of doing.

For the rest of you, who could be just as happy doing something else — you should. Success in other fields is just as fulfilling, and often easier to reach. Starting and running a good business takes a great deal of time, energy, and attention. So if being a successful entrepreneur is more important to you than working in a particular field, why not do yourself the favor of choosing a field where the competition isn't so fierce?

Since I mentioned my friend Mike, the actor, a minute ago, I'd also like to address some special remarks to those of you who may want to make a living from some form of artistic talent. You know as well as I the odds you're up against, so I won't go into all that. But I do want to tell you to run your career as a serious business.

Please, don't feel you're too sensitive and temperamental to deal with the mundane problems of ledgers and paperwork. Face the fact that even if you're the greatest painter since Picasso, the finest writer of your generation, or a better dancer than Baryshnikov, the Internal Revenue Service doesn't care.

Some fine creative careers have been hampered because talented people didn't keep good records and pay attention to the business side of their professions. Tax problems forced many of them to do any work that came their way, even if it wasn't artistically fulfilling to them, because they had to pay the government millions of dollars or face a prison sentence.

With that warning out of the way — and I hope it's a warning all my readers take to heart, whether they're creative artists or hardnosed businesspeople — let's talk about the kinds of businesses where opportunities are better.

DO THE
DIRTY JOBS

Have you ever heard the technique for coming into an organization as a stranger and quickly becoming one of the most valued, well-known members? Whether it's a corporation or a social club, the person who volunteers for the job nobody wants, and then does it well, gains everyone's admiration and good will.

Well, it's the same in business. Choose a necessary task that isn't particularly glamorous, and people will beat a path to your door. Toxic waste removal, special underwear for the handicapped, janitorial services for industrial plants, weekend business support services — you never heard of that one? I'm not surprised; but I'll bet you will.

A friend of mine told me about it recently. Curtis is an idea man, and a woman he knew came to him for advice. Betty was a secretary, but she didn't want to work all week in an office any more. She wanted to make more money, although not a lot more. What was really important to her was having time to stay home with her new baby, but her husband's salary alone wasn't enough to support the family.

Curtis thought about it for a few days, and a weekend convention where two attendees got together and started putting together a business transaction. By Sunday morning they needed their notes and a draft agreement typed up with several copies. They wanted something on paper with their signatures before they left for different parts of the country on Sunday night.

As they were telling Curtis about this over Sunday brunch, another member of their group joined their table. He was upset because he'd just learned a report he'd planned to present at the home office on Monday had a serious error in it, and needed to be revised and retyped immediately. He didn't want to miss the afternoon speeches, but it looked like he'd have to leave early and sit up all night retyping his report himself.

Curtis excused himself, went to the nearest phone, and called Betty. "Can you bring your typewriter to the hotel right now?" he asked. "I think I've just invented your new business."

Betty now works only weekends. She supplies emergency secretarial services for $50 an hour. In two days she makes more than she used to make for an entire week's work, her husband is available to care for the baby while she's gone, and she can stay home Monday through Friday.

Sounds simple, doesn't it? But Betty is doing something most secretaries won't; she works the days other people expect to be free.

Right there I can see a whole line of opportunities built on similar ideas. How about dental and medical clinics open from one in the afternoon until nine at night, enabling working people to have routine appointments without interfering with their work schedules? How many other services can you think of that are only open nine to five, Mondays through Fridays? Do you think there's enough demand to support at least one such business during evening or weekend hours?

Don't worry if you don't have the skills to actually perform the necessary jobs. You manage the enterprise and hire others to work for you. With the number of two-career families and single working parents in this country, it's past time we started opening some basic services during nontraditional hours. Say, how about evening and weekend child-care centers for shift workers? Or a landlord's credit bureau for weekend apartment hunters?

If you're more interested in manufacturing, look for something basic that's needed by consumers or by another industry. There are whole factories devoted to making one small component of larger items, from plastic control knobs to zippers. If you can develop a better model, or make something cheaper, you can get enough contracts in advance to cover your start-up financing. Sometimes companies that need what you could supply, but don't want to devote part of their own business to manufacturing the component, will even bankroll you and help you get started.

The key to any of these opportunities is research. Start with an idea, and find out who your potential customers are; or begin with a pool of customers and find out what they need. Either way you do it, the emphasis is on knowing the market. The better you know who your customers are, what they need or want, and what they're willing to spend money on, the better your chances of opening a profitable business.

A FREE IDEA

For instance, here's a free idea that comes to you courtesy of one of my editors. She tells me that for years, women's clothing manufacturers seemed to ignore the fact that half the women in America are under five feet five inches tall, and over half the women are overweight. Short women had to cut down clothes made for taller figures, which often ruined the lines. Stout women had a limited choice of unbecoming, unfashionable clothes.

Poor market research, right? Well, finally the clothing industry woke up and began making petite fashions and attractive stout sizes. There's only one drawback. According to my editor, the petite clothes — those for short women — are in pretty short supply over size twelve. And the outfits for stout women are mainly for those five foot six and taller. Again, there's a hole in the research; it's a hole just waiting to be filled by someone smart enough to realize that half the overweight women are short, and over half the short women are overweight.

Now, if I were interested in either manufacturing or selling clothes, that's a market I'd look into. I'd think up a name like "Curvy Petites" and start selling to the approximately fifteen million short stout women statistics tell us must be looking for fashionable, attractive garments. See how it works? Anyone could have arrived at that idea from either of the two directions I mentioned earlier. Someone interested in fashion could have said, "What segment of the marketplace isn't getting the clothes they want?" Elimination by various size groupings could have led them to this category.

Or someone looking first at the market could have asked, "What group has a need that isn't being filled?" Their path then might have led them to look at sex, age, and size divisions until they found this unfilled demand.

Ideas are all around you. As soon as you begin actively looking for them, you'll be surprised at how you could have ignored them before. Just be sure, once you get one, that a market actually exists, and that you have enough potential customers to make the business profitable.

LEARN FROM
THE INSIDE

Once you've zeroed in on a field you think you want to work in, you can begin actual preparation for your future independence. Naturally, you don't want to start a business you know nothing about. That's the surest route to failure. Besides, you don't want to put in your effort, time, and money until you're certain this is the kind of work you want to do.

There are all kinds of ways to learn about a field. One way, of course, is through education: classes, seminars, books, and magazines. These all have their value, and you should take advantage of them whenever you can.

Nothing, however, is a substitute for actual experience. Working in an industry you've only read about can be compared to jumping into the ocean after reading a book on swimming. No amount of study will prepare you for the wetness and temperature of the water, the force of the waves, the pull of the currents, and the challenge to your muscles.

As soon as possible, get some kind of job related to the business you want to be in. Even if it's only working in the mail room or as a secretary, you'll develop a feel for the pace and challenges of your chosen field. (Of course, you have to be alert to what's going on around you, not simply putting in your hours while you daydream about being president of the company.)

While you're working at this job, make contacts with other people. Try for as wide a range of acquaintances as possible, both within the company you work for and in the other companies it does business with. You'll learn a lot of valuable information about all kinds of things that can affect your future business. At the same time, you'll form a network of contacts to help you when you're ready for your future.

One of the best contacts you can make is to find someone to act as your mentor. This might be an immediate superior, or someone as high up the ladder as you can reach. Ideally, it would be the owner or president of the company. But if you can't get the attention of that person, go as close as you can get. You're looking for someone who knows a lot about running the business, and who is willing to share that information with you.

Sometimes you won't find that person where you work. Large companies are usually more interested in developing people to work for them than in encouraging competition. Owners of smaller businesses are often more reasonable about helping newcomers, although some of them worry about potential competitors, too. You'll have to use your judgment here. One approach is to simply express an interest in becoming more valuable to your current employer; another is to go to someone in the same business but outside the company you work for.

Once you've chosen a possible mentor, you might ask for an appointment, or invite the person to lunch or to meet with you after work. Then simply say, "I know I'm only the third assistant button-pusher to the general flunky, but I don't plan to stay at the bottom forever. I want to go places in this business. You're obviously successful, and I admire what you've done. Do you have any advice or suggestions on how I can get ahead?"

Few people can resist such a flattering approach. Even if they have to be coaxed a little in the beginning, they usually open up and tell you more than you asked for. If they don't, or if their advice proves impossible for you to follow (such as go back to school for six years, even though you've got a family to support), simply thank them courteously for their time, and go looking for someone else to help you.

A Word To
The Ladies

Women who look for mentors have to be a little more cautious than men. Although we've come a long way in the last twenty years, female mentors are still hard to find. Most industries haven't promoted many women past middle management yet; in some cases, the women who have made it to the top had to fight so hard that they aren't particularly sympathetic to other women in their field. Their attitude is sometimes, "Nobody made it easy for me, why should I help you?"

When you locate a female mentor who's willing and able to help other women succeed, you're likely to find her a combination mother, sister, cheering section, and best friend. Women who've had the experience say it's the most worthwhile, rewarding relationship of their careers. Unfortunately, it's still all too rare right now. I hope when you've become an outstanding success you'll help change this situation.

Meanwhile, of course, many women have to find men willing to act as their mentors. You must approach this situation with caution. Not all businessmen are raving chauvinists or sex-hungry wolves, and there's no reason to start out with the assumption they are. But be aware such men do exist, and try to screen them out rather than getting involved with them. To be on the safe side, don't wear provocative clothing, invite them for drinks until you know them well, or allow your relationship to get on too personal a footing.

Be prepared, too, for gossip if a female protege and a male mentor spend a lot of time together and word gets around. If you dress and behave in a businesslike manner, leave doors open when you and your mentor meet in the office, and confine your meetings away from work to very public places, you'll do a lot to kill speculation about your relationship.

The best protection, of course, is if at least one of you is very obviously happily married or involved in a well-known romance with someone else. I've known single women to wear wedding

---

rings and speak affectionately about nonexistent husbands, but be careful. The truth has a way of coming out, especially if one of the gossips has access to your personnel file.

Finally, ignore what talk may surround your relationship. Remind yourself that when you own your own business and the gossips are still stuck in the typing pool, you'll have the last laugh.

COME BACK, GENTLEMEN

Both men and women, as you learn about a particular company and form your network of contacts and mentors, should be aware of the larger industry you're a part of. Subscribe to the trade journals and business newsletters for your field. Attend seminars, read books, listen to tapes. Expand your knowledge whenever you have the opportunity. This will keep you so busy, time will pass quickly. Before you know it, you'll be prepared for the next step: going out on your own.

CHAPTER 4

YOUR OPENING MOVES

I 'm presenting these steps to opening your business as though they come in a logical, one-two-three order. Actually, as you already know, life isn't always like that. Often it seems as though we have to do everything at once.

Becoming an entrepreneur is much the same. While you're learning the ins and outs of the business you want to be in, you should also be looking at what you'll need to start your enterprise and where it will be located. Once started, there will be days when you're trying to raise financing, hire employees, fill orders, prepare tax returns, consider a new project, and still find time for your personal exercise and relaxation.

Don't worry about it. Most of us can only do one thing well at once. But that doesn't mean we can only do one thing in a day. The trick is to concentrate on a single task, do it as well as it needs to be done, and then concentrate on the next job.

You can train yourself to switch gears quickly and not waste time between tasks. Also, allow yourself an occasional breather to relax completely for ten or fifteen minutes, three or four times a day. This helps you clear your mind of details from the projects you worked on earlier and refreshes you to tackle your next project with new energy.

I mention this here because while it's necessary to write about the steps to entrepreneurhood separately, many of them are usually taken together. While you're learning all about the business you want to start, laying the foundation we discussed in the previous chapter, you'll also be turning your attention to the subjects in this chapter and the next one.

Before you can actually open the doors of your new enterprise, you'll need money, either your own or someone else's, which is covered in the following chapter. But if you want to raise money by taking in one or more partners or by borrowing, you'll need answers to some questions. Few people with the intelligence to control enough money to finance you will hand you a blank check simply because they like your style.

Instead, they'll want all the possible details you can give them about what kind of business you're starting, where it's going to be located, why you chose that location, and the benefits of locating there rather than somewhere else. In addition, you'll have to be prepared with cost and profit projections, marketing information, manufacturing specifications if you'll be creating a product, and any other facts that might affect your ability to repay the investment.

Since location is often one of the largest factors in whether businesses succeed or fail, we're going to look at that subject in some depth in this chapter. There is much more to consider here than simply where you can find enough space at the lowest price.

The first question, of course, is what kind of space do you need? Some businesses can be run handily from a kitchen table, a spare bedroom, or a garage. I know from experience that real estate investors and writers can get along just fine for years with a table, a typewriter, a telephone, and a cardboard box for files.

RESEARCH COMES FIRST

To decide what sort of space you need, where, and how much, look carefully at the profession you've chosen. Visit similar businesses and make detailed observations. Write notes for yourself so you don't forget anything important.

One of the most vital factors in choosing a location is attracting new and repeat business. Here again you'll have to know the market you plan to sell to. In fact, you'll need all the information you can get about that market. Who are your customers? Where are they? What are their buying patterns, and why will they buy from you rather than one of your competitors?

Learn your customer base. The local Chamber of Commerce and census figures can be invaluable here. Find out what sort of people live in the city and surrounding area. You'll want to know average income, the age and household patterns, lifestyle preferences. From your industry publications and marketing surveys find out what sorts of merchandise these people buy and about how much they spend.

If you'll deal mainly with other businesses, find out what and where they are, how large they are, and how much they spend annually for the goods or services you supply. You can often get this information simply by talking with the person in charge of purchasing. Explain the business you're planning, ask how much they pay their current suppliers, and tell them why you can offer a better deal.

Then look closely at similar businesses in the area. Are they busy and prosperous, doing well? Or do they open and fail regularly? During peak shopping hours, such as Saturday afternoon, watch how many customers go in and out and whether they actually buy, or simply browse and leave without spending money. Talk to the business owners if you can, and other community leaders, to get a feel for whether the area can support a business such as the one you want, or if the market is saturated.

If you can't find any businesses like the one you want to open, there are two possibilities. Either you've hit on a good opportunity, or there is not enough demand for what you want to do to support that kind of operation. Your market investigation should give you the answer to this. In addition, ask your friends and acquaintances about their own buying habits. Do they feel the local businesses answer all their needs, or would they patronize another company if it existed?

If you have any doubts at this point about whether you should go ahead with your plans, do a local survey. You can hire professional survey companies, or make up your own questionnaire. Just be sure you get enough information to help you make your decision. When you find your general location looks like a good possibility, you can start narrowing in on exactly where in town you should open.

RETAIL CONSIDERATIONS

A retail operation has to be where customers can get to it easily. Observe traffic patterns and customer habits. Do people usually shop for this kind of goods in malls or shopping districts where they can walk from one store to another? Are they willing to drive out of their way because you're supplying a specialized need? Will they know your business exists if they can't see it easily from the street? Where will they park?

Oddly enough, one of the keys to attracting business to a retail operation is often being close to the competition. Some beginners fail because they think opening their operation across town from the nearest competitor will be a smart move. It's easy to understand the reasoning behind this. If you have the only store in the neighborhood, you're bound to draw in the business, right?

Well, sometimes. But more often, buyers prefer to go where they have more choices. If all the shoe stores or furniture stores are clustered in one end of town, or along one street, or in the same mall, there's usually a good reason. Shoppers will browse for exactly what they want, going from store to store, until they're satisfied they have the best color, style, price, or whatever they're looking for. W h e n you're all alone at one end of town, certainly people who live or work near your store are likely to stop there first. If they find what they want, fine. But if they don't, or if they want to compare from a large selection, they'll head for the other end of town where all the competition is. And if they don't find exactly what they're looking for in your store the first couple of times they drop in, after a while they'll stop checking there first.

That's business. You can't please everyone all the time, and there are bound to be customers you can never suit. There's no use worrying over them. But there is something you should worry about. What about all those customers who head straight for the competition cluster and don't find what they want there?

How many of them do you think will drive clear across town on the chance they might find what they want in your one store? How many of them will even know, or remember, that there is another store? A few, maybe. But if you were right there in the mall or main shopping district with everyone else, you'd benefit from the large group who don't find what they want at your competitors' stores and try you instead. In addition, you'd be bound to catch a few shoppers who walk in to check out your store and end up buying something on impulse.

There's one important caution you need to remember about opening near your competition. If you can't be competitive with them, don't do it.

By that I mean, don't open near a store that offers much better variety or quality than you do. Generally speaking, you want to be near competitors who offer comparable merchandise at similar prices. And if you can offer higher quality, a wider selection, or lower prices, you'll have the edge.

Another tactic that works well is to open near other businesses that carry different but complementary lines of merchandise. That is, their customers will be attracted to you because what you sell goes along with what your neighbors sell.

An example of this might be a paint and hardware store next door to a tile and linoleum store. Both of you attract customers who are building or remodeling. You'll help each other, because you'll make it more convenient for people to buy several things they need for the job in one place. Some will come in on purpose to get everything, while others will go into one store and then realize after they're there that they can buy other things they need next door.

You may think I'm exaggerating the importance of this. For some kinds of retail businesses, maybe I am. If your operation is truly unique, or carries extremely high quality merchandise, people might be willing to go out of their way to shop with you. Your main problem then will be doing enough advertising to let them know where you are. It's much easier for most retail businesses to get started, though, if they're close to the areas where people already shop.

Wholesale and Manufacturing Concerns

Wholesale operations, on the other hand, need good access to their own suppliers as well as their customers. This access doesn't necessarily mean being physically close, but definitely includes facilities for shipping and traffic. Locating near a large airport and direct highway lines, on established routes used by major trucking and hauling companies, can be very important to this sort of business. Although railroad shipping is no longer as important as it once was, some industries still use it extensively. If you're involved in one of these, you'd better consider locating close to a busy rail line.

Shipping costs themselves may enter into your location decision, so consider what you'll be buying and shipping, and learn the costs. For instance, if you want to manufacture something that calls for large shipments of heavy raw material, you might be better off to locate near the sources of those materials. What you manufacture might be cheaper to ship long distances than your raw materials would be.

As an example of what I mean, here in California we have a large lumber industry. Loggers cut down thousands of huge redwoods and other big trees every year. Now, these logs are heavy and awkward. Many paper companies are located right near the logging camps, or within a very few miles of them. It's simpler, and less costly, to bring those big trees a short distance to be made into paper than it would be to move the logs halfway across the country. Paper is easier to move than logs are.

Some wholesale and manufacturing businesses find they must operate close to their customers. For instance, companies that make machine parts used by large industries often set up right next door to a major customer. This makes it easy for the customer's designers and engineers to come in and describe exactly what they want, and even watch while it's made, in some cases.

If you're planning to enter one of these fields, you've probably already noticed this pattern. You may never have consciously thought about why this is the custom, though, so be aware of it. Trying to save money by setting up your business in cheaper space can be a false economy if it means you're not convenient to your customers.

TOP LOCATION VS. COSTS

Speaking of costs brings us to another important consideration. You'll have to either buy or lease space for your business if it can't be run from your home. When you go looking, the usual rule of thumb is to find the most appropriate space at the lowest possible cost.

This may mean you have to make some trade-offs. Certainly it's important to have the best location you can find. The most desirable location, however, usually costs the most. Remember that if your business succeeds, you can always move to better quarters when your lease comes up for renewal. Against this you have to set your feeling about the importance of the location for your initial success, as well as the costs of moving later. Remember, too, that moving isn't merely trucking your supplies, furniture, and merchandise to a new location. You'll also have to change such things as signs, stationery, advertising, and order forms. Old customers will have to be notified of the move, phone numbers and directory listings may have to be changed, and your creditors and suppliers must know where you are.

All this takes time and effort from you and your staff. In addition, you'll lose more time reorganizing and getting everything set up in new quarters. Be prepared for the fact that business won't resume as usual until all these matters are taken care of, which may take several weeks.

Another factor to consider is expansion room. Is more space available if your business grows? You may soon need room for a larger inventory, more workers, or extra offices.

These are matters you're going to have to estimate for yourself. I can tell you how I handled it, which may give you some ideas, but I can't guarantee my solution will work for you.

I started out working from my home. As my business grew, I rented a small office. My business continued to grow, and it soon became apparent that I was going to need more space again. In fact, if the growth continued at its present rate, I would need a lot more space. However, if growth leveled off, I'd only need a little more space.

Finally I decided the only sensible solution was to buy an office building. I moved my seminar and investment companies into some of the offices, and rented the rest to other businesses on short-term leases. The rents I got from my tenants covered the payments on the building.

As my business grew and the leases expired, I notified some of my tenants that I wouldn't be able to renew their leases. They moved out, and my operations expanded into their former space. By that time my own enterprises were profitable enough to cover the building payments.

Today my businesses fill the entire building, and I've had to go looking for more space again. But if for some reason one or more of my companies stopped making money, I've got an alternative profit center. I'd simply close down that company and rent its space to someone else. And when I retire, I'll still own a building I can either keep as a nice source of investment income or sell.

This may not be the best solution for you, but it's worth thinking about.

WHEN GOOD SPACE IS HARD TO FIND

Of course, it's always nice when you can find exactly the building you need for the type of business you want to do. If you can't, though, there are several other ideas you can try.

Many times you can find someone with a building that's almost right for you, but not quite. Perhaps the location is perfect, but the interior is divided up into small offices when you need a large showroom. Or it's one huge room when you need a lot of private offices. If you offer to sign a long-term lease, you can usually persuade your landlord to remodel to suit you.

When the landlord wants you as a tenant, but isn't anxious to pay for extensive renovation, be creative. Offer to pay a little extra in rent, or suggest you'll allow the owner two to five percent of your net profits in addition to the rent. In effect, you're borrowing the cost of remodeling from the landlord, and then paying back the loan as higher rent or a share of profits. This can be worthwhile for both of you.

Many times, too, you'll find vacant land available in good locations. The owners of this land are often willing to build to suit a tenant. Then you can have input right from the beginning on exactly what you want. You'll almost always have to sign a long-term lease for this, though.

The length of the lease term usually varies with how specialized your requirements are. If you want something that could be easily used by a variety of other tenants, you might only have to guarantee to stay for three to five years. But when your space would be hard to convert for any other type of business, you might have to sign up for ten years, twenty, or more. In that case, you'd be wise to insist on a clause that gives you the right to sublet if you move or go out of business, or that automatically voids the lease if you close.

COMMERCIAL LEASES

Also, when you get into commercial leases, you need to know that they come in three basic forms, known as triple net, modified net, and fully serviced. Let me give you a brief explanation of these.

A fully serviced lease means the landlord pays utilities, maintenance, taxes, insurance, and any other costs for the space.

With triple net leases, the tenant pays for utilities, upkeep, janitorial service, yard care, or anything else over and above the price paid for occupancy — often including all insurance and taxes.

Modified net leases allow you to negotiate who pays for what. Where competition is strong for commercial space, the tenant usually ends up paying for more of the costs and services.

In addition, shopping center and mall leases often include a variety of interesting clauses. They may dictate how large and what color exterior signs may be, and even the shape and lettering style. Tenants are often required to spend a minimum specified amount on advertising their own stores, plus contribute to advertising the entire facility.

Shopping center and mall rents are often set as a minimum monthly fee plus a percentage of the store's profits. Also, stores are frequently required to generate a minimum amount of business, normally calculated as dollars per square foot of floorspace or linear frontage foot. When a store doesn't bring in the required minimum, the business is evicted.

BROKERS CAN HELP

You'll need to spend some time shopping around for space to get a feel for what normal charges and practices are in the area where you want to do business. Commercial real estate brokers are the people to talk to about this.

They can also help you with other facts you need, such as the zoning and business laws that will affect where you're allowed to run your operation. Occasionally you'll find the perfect location and facility, but the zoning is wrong. Or maybe you want to start from your home, but local zoning prohibits businesses in a residential area.

Zoning laws aren't set in concrete. You can usually petition your local zoning board to allow a waiver or change the zoning category if your business isn't totally unsuitable for the area. Naturally, you wouldn't open a cement plant in the middle of a residential development, or manufacture chemical explosives in the downtown business district. Check with your city offices and speak informally to members of the zoning board to learn the procedures and get a feel for how flexible your local board is.

There's one final aspect of location I'd like to mention before we go on to the next chapter. It's often overlooked by many entrepreneurs, but it has a big impact on how successful and profitable your venture will be. This aspect is employees.

LOCATION
AFFECTS HIRING

Are the kinds of workers you'll need readily available in the area? And if they are, what are their wage scales?

When you think about how important this is to your business, you'll wonder how anyone could ever overlook it. But many people who think they have an unbeatable business opportunity fail because of this one factor.

Take my friend Phil, for example. Phil had a successful printing business near San Francisco, and he raised his sons and daughter in the shop. As the kids grew up, Phil decided he could take advantage of the increasing demand for good printing and set each of his children up in business at the same time.

One of the boys got a shop south of San Francisco, and did just fine. Then the daughter opened up in Sacramento, and did great. In fact, business was so good, one of her brothers went to help her.

A few months later, looking over the records, Phil noticed the Sacramento print shop took in a lot of business from Reno, Nevada. In fact, the Reno orders could almost support a print shop all by themselves.

Phil went up to Reno and looked around. There were plenty of empty buildings in good locations at reasonable rents. The local unemployment figures indicated that while the economy was reasonably healthy, there were enough people out of work, and wages were low enough, that Phil ought to be able to run a printing business at a profit.

Naturally, Phil decided this would be a good spot for one of his boys. The one who had been helping his sister in Sacramento moved to Reno and set up a new shop. A year later, he closed it, with Phil's complete agreement.

What went wrong? It was the type of workers available, according to Phil. There were plenty of card dealers, restaurant workers, and entertainers unemployed in Reno. But there weren't experienced typesetters and pressmen.

Phil's son tried hiring promising trainees and teaching them the jobs he needed done. Unfortunately, as soon as they got some experience, they quit and moved away. Even higher wages couldn't keep them in Reno, which didn't have enough to offer anyone not interested in gambling and night clubs.

Contrast Phil's experience with the plan used by Collins Radio in Iowa. Collins had a large facility in the town of Cedar Rapids, but they wanted to open a new assembly plant. In order to control costs, they needed to put the new plant into a building with very low rent, and keep wages down. They felt they couldn't do this near Cedar Rapids, as land and construction costs were rising, and wages were going up. Research and experience indicated employees wouldn't stay on very long unless they were paid at least $5 an hour (this was in the mid-1970s).

Collins located a small town in northern Iowa where very few jobs were available. In talking with local business leaders, they learned that most residents of the town didn't want to move away from family and friends, and would usually stay if at least one member of the household had a steady job. However, wages were low, and many families included at least one unemployed person who would be happy to work for about $3.50 an hour.

To sweeten an already attractive prospect, the town offered to donate land and build a facility to Collins' specifications. This plant would be available for next to nothing for as long as Collins wanted to use it. The town was willing to do this in order to increase jobs for its residents and improve its own economy.

Happily, the plan worked out to everyone's benefit. Collins got its low-cost plant and a reliable supply of steady workers who were glad to earn what Collins could pay. The extra income was just what many local families needed to enable them to stay in their home town. And the extra paychecks were spent in local stores and businesses, which profited nicely from the arrangement.

When your business could be located almost anywhere, you can often find favorable deals like this. Look for a community that needs jobs and is willing to cooperate with you. The advantages in keeping down overhead can sometimes outweigh other drawbacks such as being farther from suppliers or distributors.

Overhead will always have to be one of your prime concerns, of course. Any decision you make about location must take this into account. Remember to figure in rent, lease, or mortgage payments, upkeep, costs of shipping in and shipping out, wages, inventory, any extra charges for warehousing or storage space, utilities, and special costs such as extra advertising or mailings to let people know where you are, or subsidies for parking facilities. The cost of your location is more than the amount of rent you pay, and all these factors have to be weighed in your final choice.

DAVE DEL DOTTO

CHAPTER 5

START-UP FUNDS

Normally, opening any sort of business takes money. Whether it costs just a few hundred dollars, several thousand, or even millions depends on the sort of business you choose.

For smaller ventures requiring very little capital, you can often come up with the money yourself. Savings, life insurance policies, credit cards, stocks and bonds, or the sale of items such as unused hobby and household equipment can often be enough to get you started.

If you need more cash, look into some of the ideas in my other books. Real estate investment can both supply you with extra money and give you valuable experience in conducting business, such as negotiating with sellers and applying for loans. Or you might prefer to go the auction route, buying everything from small household appliances to airplanes and boats for a fraction of their value and reselling them for big profits.

Friends, relatives, and business acquaintances can be another source of funds. Make a list of everyone you can think of who might be willing to loan you the money you need. You can always borrow from several sources, rather than getting the entire sum from one person.

Some people with money may not want to make you an outright loan, but would be happy to become your partner. You can draw up agreements that make you equal partners, or arrange terms that allow the other person(s) less than a half share, such as forty or fifteen percent. Your partner can be "silent," not involved in running the business, or as active as you are.

You can also set limits on the length of time you'll remain partners; you might stipulate that when your partner has been repaid his or her original investment plus a certain amount or percentage of profit for each year of the partnership, your agreement will end. Or you could say that you'll remain partners for a certain number of years, at the end of which time you can renew your partnership; one of you can buy the other out; or you'll dissolve the business and share the gains or losses in proportion to your shares in the partnership.

Partnerships are so flexible that they can be arranged in more than one form. The simplest, most familiar form is the general partnership. In this, each party has duties and responsibilities, and shares in the profits or losses, in accordance with the amount of interest that person has in the business.

The limited partnership, on the other hand, usually involves one person known as the general partner and several people known as limited partners. The general partner is in charge of actually running the business, makes decisions, and reports to the limited partners. Limited partners invest their money but have no involvement in running the business. They can, however, vote to remove the general partner if they feel he or she isn't managing their investment well.

SEEK
LEGAL ADVICE

Whenever you consider going into partnership, you should always consult a good attorney who specializes in drawing up these agreements. The attorney can advise you on the best form of partnership and will put it together for you.

The attorney can also tell you whether it's legal to advertise for a partner, or whether your particular venture, under the laws of your state, requires the parties be personally acquainted before going into business together.

This may sound like a strange requirement, but in many states, for example, it's illegal to make a public offer of a limited partnership for real estate investment unless you're registered with the Securities and Exchange Commission and submit to their regulations and controls. Failure to abide by this law can result in fines of thousands of dollars and other legal penalties.

When you enter into any form of partnership, make sure your agreement includes details on how the partnership will be dissolved if one or all parties want out. Also, provide for unexpected occurrences such as poor health, disability, and death.

If married people are involved, you should specify each partner's spouse's interest and obligations in the event of death or divorce. It would be a shame if you worked for ten years building up a business and then had to sell because your partner's spouse was awarded $50,000 from the sale of the partner's share in a divorce settlement. You might be left with the choice of buying out your partner at full cash value or selling the entire business.

Or the spouse could receive your partner's share in a settlement or inheritance, or through power of attorney in disability cases. Suddenly you're in business with someone who has no interest in or knowledge of what you do, but who may decide to hang around and poke into everything.

Instead of getting involved in situations like these, provide for them in your agreement. Perhaps you could have the option of buying out your partner's share over time, or make each other heirs in the event of death. Attorneys know how to arrange these things, so never try to draw up a partnership agreement without legal advice.

LOOKING
FOR LOANS

With or without a partner, you may want to go to an outside lender for some of your start-up funds. When you do this, you'll have to prepare a complete financial statement, and be prepared to offer collateral. Start thinking now about what you might have of value that you can borrow against. We'll cover the sorts of documents you should prepare for potential lenders and investors later in this chapter.

For a business based in and serving your community, a small local lender is often your best choice. These banks and savings and loans are interested in helping the people they live and work with, and value your account. They will probably be limited in the amount of funds they can loan, though, so if you need larger loans, you'll have to look to larger lenders.

The Small Business Administration (SBA) can be very helpful in assisting you to find loans. They also have several good books and worksheets to guide you through the process of getting permits, evaluating your business plan, and making up a prospectus and financial statement. Some of this information is free, and the rest is available at very low prices, in the range of one to five dollars for most publications.

Another source for start-up funds is venture capitalists. These are investment funds run sometimes as part of large corporations such as IBM, Dow Chemical, and Salomon Brothers. Others are funded by individuals. In either case, they are run to invest in promising new enterprises.

Some venture capital funds have strong guidelines for the types of businesses they'll invest in, while others are less particular. A few

---

confine their interests to certain geographical locations, while many others have no preference.   For instance, a recent listing for a group called U.S. Venture Partners specified they were interested in minimum investments of $1,000,000 for start-ups, companies operating one to two years with losses, and companies operating one to three years in break-even to profitable situations. Their geographic preference was northeastern and far western United States, and their industry preference was for high technology and specialty retailing.

On the other hand, the same publication stated the J.H. Whitney Co. was negotiable on the amount of minimum investments, preferred "start-ups, buyouts, other" applicants, and had no geographic or industry preferences.

A quick scan of several other entries in the same directory revealed companies stating their minimum investment guidelines ranged from "no preference" to $50,000 up to $3-5 million. Some had no preference at all on the type of project or stage of company growth, although many were looking for start-ups and companies in their first three years of business.

Geographic preferences were often open, although Venture Founders Corporation mentioned "northeast, mid-Atlantic, southeast, midwest, southwest, far west, United Kingdom, Benelux countries, continental Europe." And while many had no favored industries, a few did make statements such as "Will not consider entertainment."

Among those that listed choices, many were interested in electronics and computers, biotechnology, medical technology, and health care. There were also bids for aviation, community job generation, publishing and mail order, retailing, forestry, fishing, factory automation, service businesses, and television, to name a few.

Venture capitalists are prepared to accept the risks of helping you start a new business. Of course, they expect to profit from the successful enterprises they help finance. That's why they want to see a good solid business plan before they agree to advance you any money.

To get a list of venture capitalists, check out the June and December issues of *Venture* Magazine. If you can't find one of these issues, you can write to:

VENTURE Magazine
521 Fifth Avenue
New York, NY 10175

Mark the envelope "Attention: Back Issues" and send them a check for $5.00. Ask for the most recent June or December issue, and include the name and address you want it sent to. Inside those issues you'll find their semi-annual listing of venture capital companies.

I have no connection with this magazine, but I think it offers interesting articles and good advice for entrepreneurs, so I have no hesitation about recommending it to you.

Finally, you could incorporate your business and sell shares to raise money. This is something you should never do without an experienced attorney to help you draw up your articles of incorporation and arrange for the sale of stock.

Corporations are especially valuable if you anticipate some risk in trying to build a fast-growth company. The corporate structure protects you from personal liability for the debts of the corporation.

The 1986 tax law changes have made some corporations less valuable as a way of decreasing income tax liability; however, this may change at any time as Congress and the public overhaul the reforms. For exact, up-to-date advice on whether either a public or S corporation is the best structure for your business, the best advice I can give you at this writing is to talk to your own accountant and attorney.

PREPARING THE PAPERWORK

Now, as I've mentioned several times, the key to attracting money from potential lenders, partners, or investors is a convincing sheaf of paperwork. Some people or institutions want to see a business plan, others ask for a financial statement, and a few request a prospectus. What all this boils down to is that before you get any money, you have to prove that you're serious, that you know what you doing, and that you have a reasonable plan for paying it back, plus interest or profits.

Anyone who's at all realistic knows that not all businesses succeed, and those that fail can do so for reasons no one could anticipate or control. You aren't being asked for a one-hundred-percent, ironclad guarantee that your plan will reap unprecedented riches. You are, however, expected to show strong evidence that you know what you're doing and have taken all possible steps to maximize your chances of making a fair profit with a reasonable plan.

The way you show this is by putting down on paper an organized, logical plan for every facet of your proposed business. I sometimes compare this to the old journalism formula for a good story: 5W+H. The initials stand for What, Why, Where, When, Who, and How, although you won't call the sections of your plan by these names. Instead, give them official-sounding titles, such as "Three-Year Profit Projections and Cash Flow Analysis" or "Results of Market Survey and Opinion Research."

WHAT

"What," of course, is what you plan to do. Describe your proposed venture as completely as possible. Include everything there is to tell about your product or service, from where you'll get raw materials at what cost to distribution of the finished product through which outlets, and the final sales price. If you're retailing, describe the goods with breakdowns by categories, lists of suppliers, wholesale prices, retail markups, and expected gross and net profits.

Don't overlook payments for machinery, staff, and other overhead charges, and be sure to include the method used to divide profits. Show how much will be put back into building the business and what will be disbursed to partners, investors, loan paybacks, dividends, etc.

WHY

You'll draw on your background research into your potential market for this section. Explain why you think there's a demand for your enterprise. This could be based on one or more of several factors.

For instance, demand could be based on the needs of a certain sized population group in a particular geographical area.

Surveys in national retail publications (name the publications) state that every 50,000 suburban residents support three widget stores. Grand Town, with a population of 63,000, currently holds only one widget store, with no other competitors planning to open. Furthermore, the existing widget store has poor selection in size and color, and is slow in fulfilling special orders.

Our private survey, the results of which are reproduced on pages 18-22, indicate residents of Grand Town frequently travel to Big City or even Urban Sprawl to find a better selection of widgets. Ninety percent of widget buyers responding to our survey stated they would prefer to purchase widgets in Grand Town if a retail outlet with a suitable selection existed in their home town.

You would then go on to detail how the inventory of your proposed widget store would be better than that of the existing store.

If appropriate, you could describe how your business will fill a currently unoccupied market niche. Perhaps your research has turned up the fact that most towns with a certain square footage of office space support a particular business service which your town does not yet have. You would relate how much office space exists in your area to support this service, together with material on how local businesses respond to your suggestion that you supply this service.

This should give you the general idea. The "why" section of your plan includes all the facts and data describing why you believe your idea will succeed and how it compares to any existing competition.

WHERE

"Where" of course is your location, or locations, if you'll have multiple offices, factories, stores, or whatever. Describe the advantages of the particular location(s) — the reasons you think this is the best available place for your business.

Mention everything that has any bearing on your choice, from the convenience of shipping routes to customer traffic patterns, to facility size and rents, to parking. If the landlord has offered favorable lease terms or has room for future expansion, include that information. And don't forget to mention what labor pool you can draw from in this location if you're going to be hiring locally.

WHEN

Naturally, you can't give an exact date you plan to open unless you have a certain amount of cash or credit already lined up. However, you want to focus on any particular dates that are important to the greatest opportunity for your business to succeed.

Important dates might be those which allow you to take advantage of certain seasonal aspects of your business. For instance, if you were planning to start a specialty consumer retail store, it would be a good idea to open your doors during the summer. This would give you time to advertise and begin building a reputation and customer base before the busy Christmas buying season.

I've never run this sort of store myself, but those who have tell me they're at their busiest from about September through December. After that, business usually slows during January and February, then begins to build again toward spring. January is about the worst month for this sort of venture, so I'd advise you not to plan your opening then unless you like the idea of starting during the slack season.

On the other hand, January is a good month to launch a mail-order business. For some reason direct mail sales are best from January to about mid-May, and from September to the first part of December. You may notice your own mail increases during these times with offers for merchandise and subscriptions.

Every business has its own cycles, and you'll have to learn them as part of your preparation. Then show you've done your home-work by outlining your knowledge of these cycles and your plans for taking advantage of them when you write out your time schedule for beginning your enterprise.

Don't neglect to build lead time into this schedule. Some businesses require more preparation than others, and it's up to you to know this and plan for it. If you have to build or convert facilities, allow yourself enough time for the construction phase, including the inevitable delays. Any inventory you'll need to open should be ordered far enough in advance so that it can be in place for your official start. When you rely on particular talents or training for employees, plan to initiate your hiring phase before you'll need those people to handle important tasks.

As an example of this, I spoke recently with people who are opening a very specialized employment agency. They plan to supply businesses with highly trained skilled professionals for short-term projects. For instance, if a corporation wants to produce one training video, the agency can offer any or all the talents needed to write, film, act in, and edit the tape. Or if a company puts out one publication a year, the agency will supply everything from photographers to layout and production workers.

I think this business has good possibilities. It allows companies to take advantage of the best available pool of talent as needed, without having to keep these people on the payroll all the time. The companies don't have to sift through a pile of applications from freelancers every time they need one of these jobs done, and then take their chances that the people they choose are actually able to do the job. And it gives talented freelancers access to a wide range of opportunities they might never learn about otherwise.

The owners of the agency aren't taking any chances, though. They've spent almost a year now interviewing and checking the backgrounds of freelancers in all sorts of specialized professions, carefully building a pool of talented, reliable people. At the same time, they've prepared a careful marketing plan, targeting those companies they believe are most likely to need their services. The agency planned in an entire twelve months of lead time so that when they go into full operation, they'll be entirely prepared to offer good service to business clients and a wide range of opportunities to the freelance talent they represent.

In addition to scheduling preparation and a start-up date, you also have to project progress after your opening. This is more difficult to do, but you have to consider it carefully. Base your predictions on experiences of similar businesses and your knowledge of your market.

This is not the place to be overly optimistic. Few new ventures make a profit in their first year, and many don't break even for three to five years. Most lenders and investors know this, and are suspicious of an entrepreneur who claims to be able to go against the standard trends of an industry.

You may attract a few naive or greedy people eager to take advantage of what they see as a remarkable chance to make money faster with you than with more conservative investments. However, this is asking for trouble. It's not likely that unrealistic projections will live up to anyone's wishful thinking. When the money doesn't come rolling in as promised, your backers are going to ask questions — first of you, and then of their lawyers.

It's difficult to concentrate on business when disappointed partners, lenders, or investors are pressuring you for money. Worse yet, you may have to make payments to them from funds you need to strengthen the business. And worst of all, you could end up in court.

If an attorney can show that you attracted funds with unrealistic promises when you knew it was unlikely or impossible for the business to profit as much or as soon as you claimed, you could be convicted of several unpleasant things. Don't take the risk. It's much easier, and more pleasant, to run a solid, honest business in which you and your backers have mutual respect for one another.

WHO

It stands to reason few people with money to loan or invest want to hand it over to complete strangers. Since it's possible they've never heard of you before you ask them for funds, you have to supply them with information about who you are and why you're qualified to run your venture.

This isn't a computer dating service, however. They probably don't care that you finished second in the Mr. Muscle or Miss Prunepit competition unless your business needs an attractive or well-known spokesperson.

Of course, an exercise studio, cosmetics or clothing business, or entertainment enterprise might benefit from an owner with pleasant physical attributes. If that's the case, by all means mention it, along with how you plan to take advantage of your appearance. You could go on television, make your own commercials, demonstrate or model the product, etc. And enclose a glossy photo of yourself displaying how you plan to market the business.

For most enterprises, stick to details of your training and experience which apply directly to the business in question. Detail your years of managing a similar business, your education or special training, accomplishments or awards, knowledge of and contacts within the industry. Regard this as an expanded resume in which you explain everything about you that contributes to your suitability to run this organization.

You may not actually have all the necessary expertise. Don't try to hide it. Instead, point out the areas where you're lacking and describe how you plan to make up for these lacks. Perhaps you have a partner who can handle some of the areas you're not familiar with. Or you can hire someone to help you.

For instance, not long ago I read a prospectus written by three young men who wanted to start a computer company. One of them was excellent at computer hardware design. Another had written several successful programs for specialized business uses. A third was an expert financial manager and administrator. After detailing all their individual qualifications and accomplishments, these young men added a paragraph something like this:

None of us possess the requisite marketing skills necessary to succeed in today's competitive industrial computer industry. Therefore, we are actively seeking an experienced, highly qualified marketing manager to take full responsibility for this aspect of our business.

Those we have approached to date include [and here they mentioned several people known for their skill in marketing computers and programs, along with a brief mention of some of the accounts each of these people had handled]. The person we eventually hire must be of this caliber.

Did this paragraph turn me off, make me think these guys didn't know what they were doing? On the contrary, it told me they had a very realistic grasp of what it takes to succeed in their industry. They recognized that their expertise, while vital to the company, wouldn't succeed unless the customers knew about them. Rather than rely on their own amateur efforts to advertise, taking time and attention from their important jobs, they wanted an expert. Not only that, but they knew exactly what kind of expert they wanted and wouldn't settle for less. Now, that's professionalism.

How

Here's where you pull all your information together and give a unified, overall view of how you see your business performing over the first few years. Describe each step to be taken, along with the amount of money you plan to spend, and your projected expenses, profits, and losses.

You might want to illustrate this section with charts such as those shown on the following pages. In fact, anything in your business plan that can be presented graphically should be shown in this manner. It helps backers form a clear idea of what you have in mind and communicates your professionalism.

I can't mention too often that if you foresee any sort of problem, don't try to hide it. Admit it exists, and explain how you intend to meet it, along with alternative courses of action if your first solution fails. Successful entrepreneurs don't hide from difficult situations, but meet them head on with practical action.

FINANCIAL STATEMENTS

No request for money is complete without a breakdown of assets, liabilities, expected expenses, and a schedule for repayment. How you list some of these items will depend to some extent on the form of ownership you choose.

If yours is a sole proprietorship, your personal assets and debts must be revealed as well as your business holdings and liabilities.

WONDERFUL WIDGETS MFG. CO.

Start-up Costs

Market Research	5,000
Accounting and Legal	4,500
Deposit on Plant Lease	12,000
Renovations to Building	8,000
Electricity Deposit	200
Gas Deposit	100
Water Deposit	100
Telephone Hookup	250
Machinery	85,000
Machinery Hookup	3,000
Employee Search	1,200
Licenses	800
Office Furniture and Equipment	9,500
Systems Set-up	3,400
Total	$133,050

WONDERFUL WIDGETS MFG. CO.

Estimate of Monthly Operating Expenses

First Year Monthly Cost	Monthly Sales Forecast = $165,000 Percentage of Sales	Dollar Amount
Labor	19.5	32175
Raw Materials	24.5	40425
Rent	6.9	11385
Accounting and Legal	1.2	1980
Electricity	3.4	5610
Gas	.9	1485
Water	.4	660
Telephone	.5	825
Insurance	.4	660
Advertising	3.4	5610
Supplies	9.2	15180
Taxes	3.8	6270
Office Expense	.9	1485
Repairs	2.5	4125
Janitorial	.9	1485
Executive Salaries	10.8	17820
Misc.	1.1	1815
Total	90.3	$148,995

For a general partnership, each partner fills out a personal financial statement as well as a partnership statement. In a limited partnership, the statement concerns the general partner as well as the business holdings, but the limited partners don't ordinarily fill out personal statements. Finally, a corporation usually lists only those items which are held or owed by the corporation.

When you apply for a loan, most lenders want to see that you've put some money or other assets of your own into the venture. This makes them feel more secure. After all, if you have nothing at stake, lenders worry that you might walk away from the business when problems come up. Right or wrong, they believe you'll try harder to succeed if your money is at risk as well as theirs.

If you have nothing of material value in the business, you may have trouble getting loans. In that case, you're better off looking for a partnership arrangement. Partners usually feel they have a firmer claim on the assets of the business, and the legal right to at least oversee your management makes them feel more secure. Corporate ownership serves the same function, since corporate shares mean the shareholders have voting rights in the running of the company.

Good partners also make it easier to get loans. Look for partners who have money or other valuable assets, strong credit ratings, and dependable reputations. Then when you apply for loans, the lender can see that at least one of the parties has a good record and desirable collateral.

This is also your solution when you've had failures in the past and want a fresh start. Team up with someone who can help get the backing you need until you prove you've learned from your previous experiences.

Finally, don't lie on financial statements. If the machinery in your factory isn't paid for, state who you owe for it and how much, as well as the payment arrangements. When your office equipment is leased, don't claim you own it outright.

An astute or cautious backer will run a credit check on you, which will reveal much of this information anyway. Many lenders will ask to see your tax returns. If the investigation turns up discrepancies you can't explain, you can forget about the money.

Even if you convince someone to make a loan or invest in you without fully revealing your debts, those bills have to be paid eventually. Some people are able to use "creative accounting" to disguise where all the cash goes for a time, but the odds are pretty poor on anyone doing this indefinitely. When the truth finally catches up to you, you're in deep trouble.

Lawsuits, fines, prison, and bankruptcy are unpleasant enough, although temporary. The lasting damage to your reputation and self-respect can never be completely repaired. So stay honest; it's your most priceless business asset. Others will forgive honest mistakes, since they're part of the learning process we all go through. But deliberate deceptions create distrust about you that can limit your opportunities the rest of your life.

CHAPTER 6

CLEARING THE
GOVERNMENT
HURDLES

I told you in the opening chapter how well our country supports independent enterprise. In return, federal, state, county, and local governments require businesses to help support them.

It's a fact of life and an unavoidable part of our system. We have to pay taxes and fees to be entrepreneurs.

In addition, we must register and receive permission to do business. Some ventures require more permissions than others, but even the smallest one-person operation has to be registered somewhere.

This is part of the system of checks and balances that makes our society work as well as it does. The more apt an enterprise is to cause some harm, the more closely the government regulates individual entry into an industry. At the least, a county or city wants to be sure your business is located in an area where it doesn't annoy other residents of the neighborhood. At the other end of the scale, the law protects communities from businesses that could be extremely dangerous to the lives and health of everyone involved.

There may be times when these regulations seem specifically designed to keep you from doing what you want. Remember, though, that the intent is simply to protect the largest number of citizens. It's the same system that keeps your neighbor from doing something to harm you and your family, and the benefits to all of us outweigh occasional personal inconveniences.

Now, just what are these government regulations that affect business? They vary from state to state and town to town, so it's hard to be specific. The best I can do in a manual like this is tell you what to look for, and where to go for more information.

There are some federal rules that apply to everyone, and then I can tell you about California regulations, since that's where my businesses are based. If you understand California business requirements, those in the rest of the country will be no problem to figure out.

FEDERAL REGULATIONS

Everyone who wants to go into business must file Form SS-4 with the federal government. You can pick up a copy of this from the nearest Internal Revenue Service, and most accountants keep them on hand.

When you've completed Form SS-4 and turned it in, the government will send you an Employer's Identification Number and a kit. The kit will explain federal taxes, including Social Security, when and where to pay them, and how to figure them. From then on, you'll use your Employer's ID number when you communicate with any government agency. You'll also use it for bank and brokerage accounts and in other business communications.

In addition, certain industries are closely controlled by the federal government. These include manufacture and sales of alcohol, firearms, explosives, drugs, nuclear devices, and other controlled substances. If your business involves any of these, you'll have to apply to the appropriate federal agency.

Anyone who's planning to go into one of the closely regulated industries should learn enough about the process to know which agency regulates it. When you're in doubt, though, ask the IRS, the Labor Department, the Occupational Safety and Health Administration (OSHA) or your local senator or member of Congress.

STATE REGULATIONS

Almost all states now charge sales taxes. A quick check of state government offices in your local phone book should tell you which agency is in charge of these taxes, or you can ask an accountant. California sales taxes are collected through the Board of Equalization.

You must register with the Board of Equalization or its equivalent in the state where you do business. If you do business in several states, you may have to register in all of them.

When you sign up with this agency, you'll probably be asked to estimate your sales for the next quarter or year. Then you'll normally have to deposit a bond for your sales tax payments. This may be either an escrowed bank account for the benefit of the state, or a direct payment in cash or check.

If your projected sales tax is a small amount and you own property in the state, you might not have to put up this bond. That's a benefit to you, because any money you have tied up in the tax bond can't be used for any other purpose as long as your business continues.

Since this money is unavailable to you, it's best not to pay a larger bond than necessary. At this point, be pessimistic about your projected sales. If you're wrong, simply pay the higher tax with a smile.

You might think there's no point in registering with this agency and tying up money until you have to. Actually, though, it will help your cash flow. You see, anything you buy for resale won't have sales tax added on to it.

The state taxing agency will issue you a resale number. When you buy anything for resale purposes, give the seller your resale number and ask to have the sales tax deducted. The seller will keep careful track of this number, since it's his protection against having to pay taxes he didn't collect. (Remember, if you sell to others for resale purposes, to get their resale numbers and note them on the invoices.)

Naturally, you'll still have to pay sales tax on items you buy for use in your business, such as machinery and office supplies. Also, it's not a good idea to use your resale number to avoid sales taxes on items you buy for your personal use. Resale numbers are coded to indicate what kind of business you're in, and occasionally purchases are checked against this information.

When you register for state sales tax purposes, you'll usually be contacted by the state agency that regulates labor laws. They'll send you information on matters such as worker's compensation and other employment requirements you have to meet to hire people in the state.

In addition, if you incorporate, most states require you to register with a state corporate commission or similar agency. As I told you earlier, you should always hire an attorney to take you through such procedures, and he or she will know who to contact.

As part of this corporate registration, the state will check its records to be sure no other business in the state has the same name you've chosen. When you think you've come up with the ideal name, it's frustrating to find out someone else already has it. But it's to your benefit to make sure no one can confuse your corporation with another — and that includes creditors, unhappy customers, and IRS agents.

LOCAL REGULATIONS

Depending on where you live and what business you're starting, these may be no problem, or your greatest hurdle. The first thing you'll need is a business license. As soon as you apply for this — contact your city clerk to find out where and how — you'll usually be put in touch with the zoning and fire departments.

The fire department is concerned mainly with the safety of your venture. Does your space meet the fire codes? Are you doing anything, or storing any materials, that might constitute a fire hazard? There's very little you can do about fire code requirements, other than meet them.

At the very least you'll have to maintain working fire extinguishers on the premises and have more than one usable exit. Make sure doors and windows aren't blocked by machinery or stored inventory, and that flammable materials are kept and disposed of safely. The fire inspector will inform you, in great detail, about any other requirements for your individual premises.

Zoning is another story. Local zoning boards are made up of, and influenced by, people in the community, including those already doing business there. If they want an enterprise such as yours in the area you've chosen, you'll have no problem with them.

On the other hand, some communities deliberately try to discourage new businesses from coming in. They may already have several companies similar to yours, and the owners want to discourage competition. Or they may be in the grips of a "no-growth" movement; we've seen several of these in California recently. Residents and/or environmentalists decide a town is growing too fast, destroying open spaces and causing traffic jams, and try to put a stop to all but a few selected new businesses.

The way to deal with this problem is to find a friend with political influence. This could be your landlord, an attorney, or a powerful banker. Take time to get to know the ins and outs of local politics and choose an ally who can help you.

On the other hand, if zoning hassles and business restrictions are more trouble than the area is worth, you could simply set up your business somewhere else. Look for a town that's happy to have you, or that doesn't have a vocal anti-growth constituency.

Once you have your business license — for which you'll have to pay a small fee, by the way — some areas also require you to get an occupancy permit before you can move into business premises. Your landlord or the city clerk can tell you if you need one.

Also, if you're going to do business under a name other than your own, you'll have to file a fictitious name statement. This is often called a "DBA," for "doing business as." Again, ask your city clerk who handles applications for this.

You'll pay a small fee to file your DBA. In addition, in most towns you have to publish a statement in a local newspaper of general circulation notifying the community you intend to do business under the name you've chosen. To get an idea what these look like, check out your local paper. They usually run in very small print near the classified ad section.

The published DBA statement simply gives the name of the individual(s) who own(s) the business, the name under which the company will be known, and the location of the business. It also states the form of ownership (whether it's a sole proprietorship, partnership, or corporation) and gives a general description of the kind of enterprise it is.

If you plan to open a bank account or apply for loans in the name of the business, many banks will ask to see your DBA statement. This is their assurance that you are who you claim to be, and not some fly-by-night operator planning to disappear in a flurry of rubber checks and unpaid loans.

There. That wasn't so bad, was it? A few federal, state, and local forms, some fees and deposits, and you're ready to go. Of course, some people decide to avoid even that much hassle and simply set themselves up quietly in their own homes, without telling anyone.

The risks they run are their own. If their cover is ever blown, they can expect problems from all three levels of government, the size of the problems depending on the extent of the business and the length of time it's been in operation. The worst problems are apt to come from taxing authorities. In a community that tries to discourage new businesses, the license fees (a form of tax) may be very high. The undercover enterprise could be liable for years of unpaid fees, plus fines. In addition, if the company has sold a product without paying sales taxes, there could be all the accumulated tax and more fines. If the sums involved are very large, they might even lead to a prison sentence.

There's something else you should keep in mind about unpaid taxes. They're considered a lien against any property owned by the taxpayer. When you owe taxes to any level of government and don't pay, the arm of government in question can seize your business inventory, or your machines or office equipment, and sell them for the money to pay your tax bill.

It doesn't stop there, though. If you're a general partner or sole proprietor, the government can also take your house, your car, or just about anything else you have of value — a boat, plane, fur coat, jewelry, etc.

Incorporation can usually protect your personal possessions from this kind of seizure. Then only assets owned by the corporation can be taken. However, once you incorporate, you're registered with the state government, which means all levels of government have an avenue for learning your business exists.

Personally, I think it's much easier to simply run your business by the rules. The extra money it costs is worth it to avoid worrying about being caught. Besides, one of the most important factors in any entrepreneur's success is advertising, and how can you advertise freely if you're hoping certain people won't hear about you?

I have a lot more to say about advertising and visibility. In fact, there's so much to cover that we'll devote the next entire chapter to it.

CHAPTER 7

SUCCESSFUL

SELLING

I've said it before, and it bears repeating: Every person in
business is selling. You may be marketing a product or service
to customers; selling yourself and your ideas to potential pac-
kers; or persuading someone to work for you. Whatever the context,
wherever your company is represented, it's a sales situation.

When you're known as the head of your business, you represent
it wherever you go, to everyone you meet, even if you think of the
occasion as social or recreational. That doesn't mean you can't let
your hair down and get a little crazy with close friends from time to
time. It does mean, however, that you do your business reputation
a bad turn when you behave poorly in public.

What does this have to do with selling? It's part of your image.
And like it or not, your image sells your business — or hurts sales.

Think of it this way: Suppose you go to a Chamber of Commerce luncheon and are seated at a table with two people who run printing shops. You all exchange cards, and you notice one of the printers has a well-designed, sharply printed card. The other has an ugly logo, crooked type, and the ink is smeared. Where do you go the next time you need new business cards?

Or say, at the country club tennis tournament awards dinner, you sit between two car dealers. One of them drinks too much, spills food on his tie, complains about the price of the dinner, and says it's impossible to survive without overcharging or cutting corners. The other one drinks moderately, praises the food, and engages you in conversation, seeming interested in hearing all about you and your ideas.

Neither one of these people actively tries to sell you a car. But next time you're shopping for a new model, you're most likely to automatically check out the second dealer's lot first. Without your being aware of it, an image formed in your mind of the first dealer as an unpleasant, sloppy person, one who might try to make a few extra dollars by cheating customers.

These are small examples of the way images can help or hurt a business on an individual level. But your image starts with small, personal details and builds from there to items that will be noticed by people who never meet you face to face. It includes everything from your watch and hairstyle to your corporate logo, product packaging, and television spokespeople.

Try this. Close your eyes and think, "Coca-Cola." If you're like most people, you saw white script letters flowing across a red background, or a glass of dark brown liquid fizzing with bubbles. Maybe you even saw both. The Coca-Cola company has put a lot of money and effort into creating those images, and they're known and respected all over the world.

Chances are you've never met the president of Coca-Cola. If you did, though, and found out he was a fat man with beer on his breath, dirty fingernails, a shaggy haircut, in need of a shave, and dressed in a baggy, stained suit, what would you do? Switch to Pepsi? A lot of people probably would.

But I can guarantee you'll never see the president of Coca-Cola looking like this. Maybe his wife sees him that way, or a couple of close hunting buddies; we have no idea what his most private moments are like. You can bet, though, that he never goes out in public unless he's well-groomed and well-dressed. As president of the company, he's the world's most important Coke salesman, and he never does anything to damage the company's image. If he did, he'd be out of a job as soon as the board could vote.

ESTABLISH A PROFESSIONAL IMAGE

Of course, in creating your own image, you have to tailor it to your audience. This is another place where understanding your market will be valuable to you.

If your customers are other businesspeople, or high-income professionals with college backgrounds, your best bet is a conservative suit, good shoes, and expensive but discreet jewelry and other accessories. For more information on how to put together this look, see any of the books on dressing for success.

Lower-income customers, those whose educations stopped around the high school level, and people from non-European foreign countries, usually have slightly different tastes. Their backgrounds often include a belief that if they ever get rich, they'll let the world know it. If you want to win these people's respect, you may have better luck if you wear brighter colors, more extreme fashions, and gaudier jewelry.

Of course, if you want to sell almost anything to teenagers, the more outrageous you look, the more successful you're likely to be. Try for a blend of circus clown, bag lady, and Hell's Angel.

Seriously, watch those around you as you learn your industry. Notice who's most successful, and pattern your appearance after those people. And remember, when you go to visit a banker or government official, the discreet conservative look is best.

Once you have your own image under control, look to your business. Everything about your premises should reflect your professional ability and commitment to success.

This does not necessarily mean lavish offices and expensive furniture. As I mentioned in Chapter Two, entrepreneurs who run their businesses profitably don't waste money on useless extravagances. If it's important to your image with customers or backers to present a luxurious atmosphere right from the beginning, of course, then you need it. But ask yourself if it's really because your business demands it, or your ego.

Even companies that don't usually need offices can still look good. Keep the premises neat, as far as possible within the limits of the job. Clean machinery and well-kept tool racks, with everything not in use put back in a designated place, helps present a good image in shops and factories. Items not in frequent use should be kept in closed-off storage, not piled in a corner. And someone should sweep up and dispose of litter every day, even if that someone has to be the owner.

Of course, maybe you won't have an official place of business to begin with. You might be starting out of a corner of your living room and a briefcase. There's nothing wrong with that; but when you have to meet with clients, it sometimes presents problems.

It doesn't look completely professional to invite business associates to your home, particularly if members of the family are on the premises. Other adults may be persuaded to leave for a while, or at least stay in another room; but children and pets aren't always so cooperative. If this gets to be a problem, there are several solutions.

Some people use a booth in a convenient coffee shop as their office away from home. It isn't always necessary to admit that's what you're doing. You can simply say something like, "I haven't had lunch yet, why don't we meet at the Brimming Cup and talk there?"

Others borrow office space from a friend or business acquaintance. This can even be arranged by paying an hourly rate for the time you need the space.

Many larger towns and cities present this option on a more formal basis. You can find office buildings that rent offices and conference rooms by the hour or day. Most such businesses ask you to pay a minimum monthly fee, which entitles you to a certain number of hours per month. For any time over that, you pay extra.

These as-needed offices can work well while you're in transition, not ready for a full-time office but needing one several times a month. They usually also supply mail service — where you have your mail sent to their address and pick it up or have them forward it to you. Secretarial service, answering service, and parcel and express mail shipping are also often provided by these firms. To locate them, simply look in the Yellow Pages under "Office — Desk Room Rental" or "Secretarial Services."

If it's so simple to get temporary office space as you need it, do you really want to rent a full-time office? Eventually, yes. These temporary services normally charge more than the going rate for comparable permanent quarters. As you need more and more office time, you'll find it's much more economical to set up in your own place.

Besides, there are other considerations. As most businesses grow, they generate records and files that must be kept in one central location. The busier you become, the less you'll want to leave your work site to meet people in coffee shops or someone else's office. The temporary office is a handy tool for part-time and start-up businesses, but when you're successful, you usually want the time and money savings of having a permanent office.

YOUR PAPER IMAGE

This brings us to an aspect of image that I've lumped all together, even though some of the pieces may need to be in place before you're ready for a permanent address. I'm talking about such items as signs, stationery, logos, trademarks, and business cards.

Some people believe they can save money by designing their own signs, logos, etc. That may be true; but I'm inclined to think it's a false economy. You don't have to spend thousands of dollars having a distinctive logo researched and designed. You should, however, hire a professional graphic artist to do this for you, unless you or someone you know is actually a professional in this line. By that I don't mean a student, or a talented amateur, but someone who regularly earns money for this kind of work.

I may sound a little fussy about something that appears to be a small detail, but it's really important. Your sign, your card, or your stationery may be the only part of your enterprise many business contacts ever see. Even if they eventually come to your store, factory, or office, the initial impression they'll get of you and your company will be from your advertising and stationery. You want that impression to be the best it possibly can.

So hire a professional to design a logo for you. You don't have to get the best, most expensive artist in town, but get someone with a good reputation. Many beginners charge very little for this kind of work, but do a good, professional-quality job.

Your logo may include a picture or symbol as well as the name and address of your company in distinctive, attractive type. Then use this logo everyplace you put your business name. It goes on your stationery, cards, signs, invoices, advertising, and checks.

The individual look of your logo helps people remember your company's name from one time they see it to another. It's an important part of your image, so choose your design carefully and don't change it often.

"REAL" SELLING

The next step in building your image is the part most people think of as "real" selling. This is the wide range of activities referred to as marketing and public relations. Many, many books have been written on these subjects, and there's no way I can make you an expert on it here. All I can do is point you in some directions for further research.

While you need to know and understand your target market for many reasons, advertising is the place you absolutely can't afford to guess. You must have a good idea who your customers are and how to reach them.

Do they watch television? If so, what programs, during which hours of the day? When do they listen to radio, and what stations do they favor? Do they read *People, Wall Street Journal, Playboy, Forbes, New Yorker, National Enquirer, Cosmopolitan,* or *Mother Earth News*? What trade journals or newsletters do they subscribe to? Do they order by mail, or do they prefer to shop in person? Do they buy only for themselves, or do they purchase gifts, items for an entire family, or supplies for a whole company?

You see, there are so many advertising media, and so many ways to use those media, you have to know what you're doing before you spend money on any of them. Money spent on the wrong advertising is money lost — money that could have been used for the right advertising.

Even such a simple matter as choosing a listing for the Yellow Pages depends on knowing your market. If you're competing for consumer dollars within a limited geographical area, it's wise to spend money on a display ad, one that shows your logo and tells a little about your business. But if you're going after a specialized national market, keep your Yellow Pages listing small and spend more on a vehicle that reaches your target group.

Once you know who you're trying to reach, advertising departments will help you. When you're considering television, radio, or print media, ask the advertising or commercial sales department for rate cards and survey profiles. These tell you the charges for different sizes or lengths of ads, and break down viewers, listeners, or readers by several categories.

Typical survey profiles include age and income ranges, sex, marital status, number of children, spending habits, special interests, and a variety of details. You can get this information for the cost of a letter or phone call and study it to see if these people sound like good customers for you.

When you locate good ad markets, how do you approach them? Often this involves decisions between ideal advertising and what you can afford.

The important thing is to catch people's attention. After all, you can't tell them how great your product or service is if they don't read, watch, or listen to your ad.

In print media, this usually means the largest ad you can afford, one with visual impact. A picture of your product, a bright color, or some large, attention-grabbing lettering helps here.

Radio presents a different challenge. The appeal is to the ear, so your ad has to say something in a unique way. Catchy music, interesting dialogues, short snappy slogans, and sometimes suitable sound effects can make the listener remember your business.

Television combines both these techniques. The viewer needs

something to look at as well as listen to, and it has to make a vivid impression. After all, your ad is competing against the refrigerator, the bathroom, family or friends, and whatever's on the other channels.

Other forms of mass-market advertising include flyers and direct mailings. You can often distribute flyers in a limited area, either by yourself or hiring youngsters to take them around for you. This is a cheap, quick method to reach a large group of people, but it's fairly random, as the people receiving them will typically be all residents of a neighborhood, or people who park in a particular lot.

Direct mailings allow you to narrow in more on your market. List brokers and subscription lists offer survey profiles and usually can supply figures on how successful other mailings have been to the same lists. You can rent lists from other mail-order companies, magazines and newsletters, and through direct mail brokers. Find list brokers in most major population areas by looking in the Yellow Pages under "Direct Mail." Once you start advertising, other brokers will contact you.

For direct mail, a two percent response is good. That is, for every hundred flyers or envelopes you mail, two people will order. This means you must watch costs closely to be sure you can break even with fewer orders. Keep track of your costs for developing and printing your ad, postage, envelopes, list rental, and the cost of fulfilling the order, including labor, boxes or envelopes, and shipping costs.

Many mail order businesses start by placing ads in the classified sections of national newspapers and magazines. The general rule of thumb is that it's difficult to sell anything for more than two or three dollars through these ads. Therefore, if you're selling something more expensive, the common practice is either to pay more for a larger ad, known as a display ad, or to run a small classified ad offering free information. Those people who reply are sent a packet containing a detailed brochure or long flyer, along with ordering information.

Also, if you sell by mail, be sure to keep a list of those people who buy from you. Later you can send them advertising and catalogs for other products. In addition, you can rent your list of names to other direct-mail sellers. Typical rentals average around $40 to $60 per thousand names, so a few thousand names can earn you several hundred dollars a month. Just be sure your list isn't rented to your direct competitor.

DIRECT SALES METHODS

Some products can be sold more effectively through direct customer contact. If you manufacture one or only a few items that would be suitable for some sort of store, but don't want to open a retail outlet yourself, try getting your products into other people's stores. Talk to owners of small individual outlets, or buyers for large chains (contact the chain's nearest office to find out where the buyers are).

Some stores, especially the smaller ones, may not want to buy from you outright. In that case, offer to leave a few samples on consignment. This means if they sell, the store collects the money, keeps a share of the price, and gives you the balance; if they don't sell within a certain length of time, you'll take them back and the store pays you nothing.

Occasionally you'll find an item that sells best if someone demonstrates its use. In this case, you can arrange to supply a demonstrator — many temporary employment agencies can send demonstrators — as well as any special equipment needed. You pay all costs for the demonstration, and the store handles all sales, paying you your share from their profits. This is also a good technique to use for trade shows and conventions.

You shouldn't regard demonstrations as a regular part of your sales campaign, however. They're valuable for launching a new item, or for drawing attention to a product that's good for a particular season. However, word of mouth and other advertising has to be able to carry the product after the demonstration.

If that doesn't work for you, you may have an item that's best handled by a sales staff. Since salespeople work on commissions, you'll share some of your profits with them. It's worth it though, since without them, you'd lose many sales.

Salespeople can also give you valuable firsthand insights on the types of customers who like your product, what they like best about it, and the criticisms of those who don't buy. This allows you to tailor your other advertising, product development, and future sales campaigns so that they target your best markets and overcome the objections of those who didn't buy in the past.

You can send your sales staff to individual homes or businesses, but this isn't always efficient. In recent years the trend has been more to let customers come to the sellers.

For business items, this means sending sales staff to conventions, trade shows, and meetings of business associations, where they can contact a preselected pool of most likely buyers. Consumer goods, especially those directed at women, sold well through the home party system for many years. I'm sure you're aware of how that works. One woman, the hostess, invites several of her friends over for an evening. They have refreshments, perhaps play a game or two, and someone demonstrates kitchenware or cosmetics, or displays clothing, then takes orders. The hostess receives free merchandise, the value and quantity depending on total sales for the evening, for the use of her home.

In recent years the home party system has suffered. The increase in two-career couples and single mothers makes it more difficult to persuade several busy women to all get together on the same night.

Several innovations have developed to overcome this problem. One is to designate one woman as hostess, and have her supply a list of friends who are interested in the product. The salesperson then visits these people individually and takes their orders. The woman who supplied the names still receives a hostess gift.

Another is to turn the salesperson's home into a showroom. He or she sets up a display and demonstrates products to anyone who comes by during designated hours. This has also been combined with the hostess system, asking someone to invite all her friends to stop by during a week or ten-day period, and giving her a gift for their orders. I have no doubt other variations will come along as American ingenuity finds new ways to conduct business regardless of changes in society.

Finally, the most recent development in home consumer contact is the field of telemarketing. This involves reaching customers by telephone. There are also several ways to do this.

One of the least complicated is to invest in a computerized calling machine. This machine can be programmed to call all the numbers with a certain three-number prefix, or every third number, every fifth number, or whatever you like. It then goes through all possible combinations for phone numbers following that prefix, starting with 0001 and going up to 9999.

When someone answers the call, the machine plays a pre-recorded message advertising whatever you're selling. It then tells the person to respond with a name and phone number, and perhaps a time of day, for more information on the product or to place an order. There is blank tape for the person to reply. Later, you can play back the tape and call everyone who expressed interest. (Some states now require a live person to come on the line before the recorded message plays and introduce the company's name, then ask if the person who answered the phone will listen to a recorded message. To find out whether this applies in an area where you want to use your machine, call the local telephone company's business office.)

If the machine gets a busy signal, or no answer, it will simply go on to the next number, while keeping a memory of the number it missed. Later, it goes back and retries all those numbers, up to as many as three times, or until it gets an answer.

Unfortunately, this system has one drawback. Many people are annoyed when they answer the phone and find a machine on the other end. If you're concerned about turning off these people, you might prefer hiring human beings to make your calls.

Many large cities now have companies that specialize in telemarketing. They'll take on almost any product for you and assign a crew to make calls to random numbers or specialized lists. You may have to tell them what to say, although some companies employ experienced people who can write a script for the callers to use.

Or, you might prefer to hire your own crew. You'll have to pay the telephone bills and supply them with some space, but if the campaign is at all successful, you'll save money. You can write their sales pitch yourself, hire an expert to do it, or let the crew members make up their own scripts. I'd suggest, though, that you at least give them an outline of what they should cover in their conversations. Telephone salespeople can work simply on commission, or on salary advances deducted from future commissions.

GETTING YOURSELF NOTICED

In addition to all these forms of paid advertising, there's also what I think of as "free" ads. These aren't actually free, since it takes at least a little money to get them, but payments aren't made to the radio or television station, newspaper, or magazine that spotlights you or your business.

Our entertainment and information media are always looking for new subjects, interesting personalities, fresh ideas, and business innovations. Not only that, but specialized programs and publications need a constant supply of material about the subjects they cover. That's where your publicity and press release campaign gets you attention you couldn't buy.

Make up a press kit or publicity release about yourself, your business, or your product, and send it out to everyone who might do a story on you or your business. Public libraries have books with the addresses of television and radio stations and newspapers all over the country, along with the size of their audiences. To find them, just tell the reference librarian what you need.

If you're starting small, you'd mail to your local papers, the nearest big-city paper, local television and radio stations, and magazines directed to the same markets you want to sell to, as well as those within your own industry.

For instance, if you're manufacturing the first purple plastic widgets, you'd notify magazines bought by widget customers, the *Widget Builders' Monthly* trade journal, and perhaps a plastics journal. You'd also contact the cable television company that produces "Widget Week" (a look at new industry developments), your local community access TV program, and the radio show that features local business news, as well as the editor of the newspaper business section and perhaps a reporter who often writes features about unusual goings-on in your town.

Direct your mailing to suitable people at each address. Target particular programs at radio and television stations, ones which routinely report on or interview people with stories like yours. For publications, write to the editor in charge of the department, or departments, most likely to be interested.

For example, when I send releases to newspapers, I usually mail them to real estate editors, since real estate is my primary business. But I might also send them to the book review or entertainment editor if the information concerns one of my books or television shows. And on my hometown paper I'll contact the feature editor as well, since there's a "local boy makes good" angle to the story.

A publicity release is usually only one or at the most two pages, typed double spaced on one side of the paper. You can also send a picture with it, either of yourself or your product or place of busines. Make sure it's interesting and clear, and be sure it's a black-and-white glossy. (Eight by ten inches is a good size, although you can also use a four by five.) Attach a label to the bottom or back to identify the picture; never write on the back, as this can show through and ruin the photo.

A press kit also contains a publicity release of up to three double-spaced pages, plus some background information on you or your company, and a brief one-page biography of yourself. You should include at least one eight-by-ten glossy photo of whatever is most interesting about your company, or of yourself if you're the focus of interest. You can send two or three pictures if you want, but these are costly, and normally if any pictures are used, only one will be chosen. The rest will probably end up in the trash, so think twice before you spend a lot of money on extra photographs.

The press kit can also contain any other items you think will help to tell your story, including mention of other media which have featured you, copies of articles about you, or a schedule of appearances you plan to make. (This is helpful if you plan to be in a certain city at a specific time and want to schedule several interviews during that time.)

You may put everything into an envelope, or enclose the papers and photo in a presentation folder. Companies with large budgets often design fancy folders, coordinating the outside color with the color of the letterhead they use on the press release, and enclosing glossy brochures advertising their products. Some even include free samples, if it's something small.

Experienced media people aren't particularly impressed by this. They enjoy the pretty colors, and appreciate the samples if they're useful. But their primary interest is in whether or not there's a good story or interesting interview here. If there's not, the fancy brochure goes in the wastebasket along with the color-coordinated stationery. The expensive folder may be used to file notes for the story that is chosen, or end up on Junior's history report.

As long as it's neat and legible, your release stands a good chance of attracting attention, with one big if: If there's a good story in it. To interest the media, you have to offer news or entertainment. Lead off your press release with the most interesting or intriguing information about your story, or a controversial quote.

Media people love controversy, as long as it doesn't get them sued. If you can think of a way to work it in, draw attention to it. Instead of beginning your release with a sentence like, "Joe Blow's new factory is different because it allows the workers to choose their own hours," try something like this: "We're going to change the way everyone in this country does business," states Joe Blow, president of Amalgamated Widget, Inc.

Emphasize whatever is new, different, strange, or particularly interesting about your company. Maybe you hire the handicapped, and your lead foreman is a woman in a wheelchair. You may have found a way to let buyers design their own product. You could be one of the few women in a man's field, or a man in a woman's industry. What do you do that's unique, first, bigger, better, newer, more original?

Everyone has something. It could even be your hobby. I've recently seen stories about a contractor who sings opera, a clown who carves duck decoys, a corporation president who plays Santa Claus at orphanages, and a skydiving fashion designer. These stories first attract attention, then slip in a mention of the subject's business.

This is the place to show off your Miss Prunepit or Mr. Muscle title, particularly if it contrasts with the type of business you're in. "Former Beauty Queen Makes Fortune in Sewage" or "Muscleman's Quilts Win Art Prize" are the types of stories few editors can resist.

DO-IT-YOURSELF
— OR NOT?

When you start advertising, should you do it yourself, or hire professionals? There are two ways of looking at this. Naturally, since it's your business, you know more about it than anyone. But do you have the skills to do a good job of advertising, and the time to handle it plus tend to your business?

Obviously, if you're starting out on a very slim budget, you may have to do your own ads at first. Paying for additional ads may be more important than paying someone else to write and place them for you. The problem with this is that if you aren't very good at advertising, you may not make enough money to ever afford a professional, or even to stay in business.

If you simply don't have the money, then you have no choice. But do yourself a favor and at least read some books on advertising. Take a course in marketing if it's at all possible.

You may find you have an unexpected flair. There are some classic examples of company owners who went on television to advertise their own businesses. Most of them did it to save the cost of hiring professional writers and announcers. To their surprise, customers loved it and responded so strongly that now these businessmen wouldn't consider hiring anyone else to represent their companies.

That's one side of the story. The other side is that a good many very intelligent, astute businesspeople don't have much ability for advertising. Their talents are in organization and management, or product design, or raising money, or whatever the basis of the business may be. If you're one of these, don't worry about it. Spend your time where it will benefit your enterprise the most, and hire someone to handle advertising.

You don't have to start out with an expensive full-time staff and a marketing manager. Contact an agency, or hire an individual freelancer to write or produce one ad or press release. If you like it, use it over and over. If it doesn't work as well as you'd like, have it redone. And if the person who's doing it can't seem to get it right, go to someone else.

In choosing someone to work on your marketing campaign, get referrals from others in your line of business. Find out who they like and feel does a good job. When interviewing an agency or freelancer without referrals, ask to see samples of their work, and ask for references.

Be particular. This is one of the most important choices you'll have to make. Your sales and profits, and therefore the entire future of your company, depend on good advertising. Get the best people you can afford to handle it.

OPEN YOUR
OWN AGENCY

When you or a member of your staff handles all your advertising, you should start another business. You see, advertising agencies receive a commission on ads they place for customers in many publications. This is usually fifteen percent. When someone who isn't affiliated with an agency places the same ad, he or she pays the same price, but doesn't receive the commission.

You can designate your advertising department as an in-house agency. Set it up as a separate arm of your company, with its own name and letterhead. If you're Amalgamated Widget, this could be as simple as Amalgamated Widget In-house Advertising Agency. Then, when the business submits advertising copy, ask for the in-house agency discount. The price of your print ads will be reduced by fifteen percent in a number of publications.

As I said at the beginning of this chapter, there's no way I can tell you everything about advertising in a few pages, or even an entire book. But I hope I've given you some ideas and information you can use as you set out to educate yourself. Let's go on now to look at some things you'll need to know about actually starting operations in your new career.

CHAPTER 8

OPERATING YOUR NEW COMPANY

E ntrepreneurs are usually active people who like to make things happen. This is a plus when it comes to starting companies and getting new ideas off the ground. But as with most characteristics, there are times when this trait has to be kept under control or it could cause unnecessary problems.

You see, I've noticed that a good many entrepreneurs, faced with almost any task, will jump right in and start doing it. And they don't have much patience with other people who don't react the same way. The typical entrepreneurial attitude could be stated as, "I don't care how you do it, just get it done."

Many times, this works perfectly well. With a lot of chores, it doesn't much matter whether you lay out an organized, step-by-step plan for the most logical way to proceed before you start. The important thing is to complete a series of actions, in almost any order, and keep going until you're done.

As an extremely simple illustration of this, suppose you're making one sandwich for yourself. Whenever you feel hungry you spread mustard on the bread, slice the meat, add mayonnaise, cut up a tomato, sprinkle on some salt, and tuck in a lettuce leaf, in almost any order. The only objective is to get everything you want between two slices of bread.

But if you're running a sandwich shop where you make a couple of hundred sandwiches between 11:30 and 1:30 every day, you're probably going to approach the process a little differently — you'd better, if you don't want the lunch hour to be a daily disaster.

Very likely you'll start a couple of hours before the lunch rush. You'll slice all the beef, then all the ham, then all the turkey, and so on. And you'll arrange a work area with the assorted ingredients lined up in order so you can spread mustard and mayonnaise, add meat, toss on the tomato and lettuce, and be ready to start the next order with minimum wasted time and motion. You may even make up a selection of the most popular sandwiches ahead of time.

It's all a matter of scale. When you're doing something simple, with no pressing time constraints, you can afford to muddle through without paying attention to which details come in what order. But when you run a business, or do anything of any complexity, it's wise to stop and analyze practically every aspect of it. The best time to do this is at the beginning, before you or your staff establish any sort of routine.

Is routine necessary at all? Some free spirits like the idea of walking in and jumping into whatever they're in the mood to handle first. When that's done, they look around to see what they feel like doing next, and so on through the day.

That may work for some people, and some enterprises, but for most of us and most businesses it isn't very productive. For one thing, certain tasks have to be handled at particular times. If your ad copy has to be at the printer on Wednesday, you can't simply trust that you'll be in the mood to work on it before then. You must set a time to start, and be sure it's early enough to finish the job even if you run into unexpected problems or are interrupted.

Bank deposits have to be made before bills are paid, and somebody has to sit down and do the bookkeeping. If you aren't in the mood, the unpaid bills and bouncing checks could ruin your credit rating. Businesses with poor credit don't last very long these days.

Without a routine, some jobs won't be started early enough. Worse yet, very likely a few jobs won't get done at all. No matter how much you love what you're doing, there's almost certainly at least one task you hate to face — answering mail, talking to the bank about a loan, hiring or firing employees, taking inventory, learning how to use a computer.

You can make up your own list; these are just the answers I got when I asked a few friends what they liked least about their businesses. The point is, when you only do those things you feel like tackling, some jobs never get done, because you never feel like doing them. And the longer you put them off, the easier it is to forget they need doing.

There are some other problems with being disorganized. Even if you get around to doing everything, without established systems, the tasks will be done in a haphazard manner. That means they may be done poorly, with loose ends and unfinished details. Also, you're apt to waste time and energy that could be used to complete the job you're doing plus another one besides.

When you add other people to the picture, it looks even worse. If you don't have a system for what you're doing, your employees get confused. They waste time waiting for you, or interrupt what they're doing to take care of something else you've decided they should do instead. Then they lose track of where they were on the original task, and lose time going back to pick up the threads. In the process, they sometimes forget details, or think they finished something they haven't.

Some entrepreneurs believe the answer is to hire a few department heads — or one-person departments — and let each of those people organize their own individual tasks. Not true! The person in charge of a job or department will arrange things to suit him- or herself. This may or may not keep the department running smoothly; it depends on the organizational talents of the person in charge. But even if each department runs well, it's no guarantee the different departments will interact for the most successful running of the entire company.

A Cautionary
Tale

To demonstrate what I mean, let me tell you about the company a friend of mine *used to* own. He sold products by mail. My friend, Tom, was a really nice guy. He was also a typical entrepreneur, full of energy and bright ideas, and impatient with details.

Tom's company grew from a one-man operation to the point where he had several employees. At first, Tom and a secretary took care of everything. As the business grew, he hired someone to help with shipping. Next, he got a part-time bookkeeper, and then he hired an assistant to help him find new products and handle advertising.

Within three or four years, Tom's business was thriving — at least on the surface. Orders rolled in at a satisfactory pace. He had a product manager, in charge of locating and negotiating for new items to sell; an advertising manager; a bookkeeper; a computer operator; three people in shipping and receiving; and a secretary who also handled customer service. Tom only had to come in a few hours a day, and could take off several weeks in the summer and again during the winter.

What Tom didn't realize until later was that just as the business seemed to become exactly what he wanted, it was actually reaching the breaking point.

In the beginning, when Tom and his secretary did everything, they failed to set up any systems. Tom decided what needed to be done next, and either did it or delegated it to the secretary. As new people were added, Tom showed them how he'd done things in the past, and then left it up to them to handle their jobs in their own ways. As long as the business continued to make money and no big problems came up, Tom figured everything was all right.

Actually, trouble was brewing in every department. When the secretary received customer complaints, she passed them along to the shipping department. The people there, having no idea what to do with them, simply stuck them in a box and forgot about them.

The people in shipping also arranged the inventory so they had the maximum number of excuses to leave their work stations and wander around. They didn't stockpile cartons of products around the packing tables. Instead, they filled each order individually, strolling through the warehouse with the order slip in one hand and a basket in the other, stopping to visit when they came across each other.

Also, the shipping people never reported when they were getting low on a particular item, but only told someone when they had sent out the last one. Then backorders piled up until a new supply arrived. Only sometimes it didn't arrive for weeks, and occasionally the item turned out to be unavailable. Meanwhile, unfilled orders were filed under the name of the item they were awaiting.

Unfortunately, some of these orders were waiting for more than one out-of-stock item. But they were filed under only one of these. It sometimes happened that other items on those orders came in, but weren't sent to the customers because the order wasn't cross-filed to each out-of-stock purchase on the invoice.

The product manager and the advertising manager communicated occasionally, but not well. They talked about what products might be available in the future, and what the advertising deadlines were, and then went their separate ways. If the advertising man thought one of the items sounded like a particularly good seller, he'd put it into a catalog or flyer with several other products. He didn't check back with the product manager, who in turn didn't notify him of product status. Several times these ads were mailed out when the new item wasn't available to the company, or was delayed in production. This resulted in customer complaints and unfilled orders — which disappeared into those files in the shipping room.

Meanwhile, the bookkeeper tried to cope with an accounting system that didn't answer anyone's needs. No separate funds were set aside to cover advertising bills, or salaries, or to pay product suppliers. Whichever bills were most pressing got paid.

Frequently the bookkeeper promised payment to someone and then Tom ordered a check to be sent to someone else instead. When suppliers and advertising media demanded money at the same time, Tom told the bookkeeper to pay them both — and sometimes the checks bounced. The company lost credit privileges with several accounts, and then was often pressed to come up with cash for needed ads or products.

The staff expressed their concerns to Tom, but he solved problems with temporary stopgap measures. Rather than set up systems so the same problems wouldn't occur again in the future, he took care of immediate crises and then forgot about them.

Among themselves, Tom's staff decided they needed regular meetings to advise each other of current and ongoing developments in each of their departments. They told Tom they wanted at least a weekly meeting of department heads, and that they thought Tom should attend as well. Tom replied that he didn't think the company was large enough to need such meetings, but he would allow them to try it if they thought it was necessary.

The entire staff attended the first meeting, except for the secretary. Everyone learned some interesting facts about functions in other parts of the company that they hadn't realized were problems. For instance, the shipping people complained that order forms were often designed in ways that made it unnecessarily difficult and time-consuming to fill orders. Also, they wanted to be informed when big sales campaigns were due, so they could be prepared. Several times they had been surprised by large influxes of orders when they were short of boxes and shipping labels, which took several days to order and have printed.

The next week Tom didn't attend the meeting. He said it was a waste of his time, and that the staff could handle their conferences without him. However, several people wouldn't accept suggestions or new assignments from anyone but Tom. No problems were solved at that meeting, and it soon degenerated into a general gripe session.

Staff meetings continued for several weeks, but without Tom's authority to approve and order solutions, they didn't accomplish much. Each person became aware that problems they thought were peculiar to their own department were reflected in all the other areas of the company. This led to increased frustration, and the employees began to think of the entire business as a disorganized mess they could never straighten out. Morale suffered, and some key people started looking for other jobs.

Within a year, all the department heads quit and were replaced by less experienced people. But even then Tom either didn't recognize that poor organization was the root of his problems, or else was unable to do anything about it. He chose to believe his previous employees were incapable of handling their jobs, and expected their replacements to do better.

What actually happened was that the new people were even less able to cope. They hadn't had the experience of coming into the company earlier and learning their way around while it was smaller. They also didn't have the resource of more experienced workers who could help them understand their jobs and the company; those people were gone.

Quality control suffered as the new workers struggled to learn their jobs and try to keep business going in their disorganized environment. Customer complaints increased, but there were still no systems to handle these properly. Eventually the inevitable happened; dissatisfied customers began filing lawsuits, and some of them complained to the Postmaster General.

Tom tried desperately to keep his business alive in the face of steadily increasing chaos. Employees quit almost as soon as they understood what was going on, so that Tom was constantly trying to find people to help him. Advertising fell off as credit dried up. Orders tapered off as a result of less advertising and spreading customer dissatisfaction. Product manufacturers hesitated to commit merchandise to a company with poor credit and a bad reputation.

The strain began to show in Tom's face, but he wasn't ready to give up. He was determined to turn his business around and make it successful once more. But the effort was made more difficult by the amount of time he had to spend talking to lawyers, appearing in court, and sitting through audits.

He took out a second mortgage on his house, and then a third, and put the money into the business. The extra funds helped for a month or two, but it wasn't enough. After months of nightmarish struggle, Tom's business went completely broke, and he lost his house as well. To finish a sorry tale, the stress and worries caused Tom's marriage to fail.

YOU DON'T HAVE TO
BE ANOTHER TOM

This is a true horror story. Sadder yet, it isn't unique. I personally know dozens of people who have had similar experiences, and have heard stories of hundreds more.

Boiled down to their essence, most of these unhappy tales have the same basic facts in common. An energetic, optimistic person with a good idea gets a company up and running. However, being a go-get-'em entrepreneur who has no patience with details, the company's founder doesn't establish orderly systems. He or she fails to make sure every department of the growing business has a logical, efficient routine, and that these routines all intermesh smoothly with the running of each other area of the business.

You can hire efficiency experts and organizational consultants to come in and analyze your business to establish procedures for you if you can't handle these details yourself. Or you can do it yourself.

Look at each task performed. Ask yourself, who is affected by this task? Who else should know about it? For example, if you're acquiring or manufacturing a product, advertising has to know when it will be available and what benefits will appeal to customers. Sales and distribution people need time to plan how they'll offer the product to customers, and when to promise delivery. Warehousing and shipping departments might need to clear space for new inventory or order a supply of special packing.

Customer service has to know enough about each product to explain it to customers who have problems. There should also be clearcut procedures for dealing with specific complaints: refunds or credits, replacements, etc.

In addition, customer service should describe particular kinds of problems to different departments. Confusion about how to use the product might mean advertising, salespeople, or instruction manuals must communicate more clearly with customers. Frequent breakage and shipping damage should be reported to warehousing and shipping people, who should investigate and change any of

---

their procedures that cause such damage. The same problems should also be reported to production or to merchandise buyers, so that they can look at the design and manufacture for flaws, and consider changing or dropping the product.

You see, a business isn't completely a group of independent workers all concentrating on specific tasks. Everything is interrelated. Once a business is running, someone has to step back and watch the big picture. It's a manager's responsibility to make sure all the parts mesh smoothly and that problems aren't hidden or unrecognized.

Maybe management isn't your strong point. That's all right. You can learn to do it better, or hire managers. But no matter who's doing it, the key point to remember is that every decision must be made with benefits and drawbacks for the entire company in mind.

LEARN TO BE YOUR OWN
EFFICIENCY EXPERT

To analyze your systems, or lack of them, look at each task performed by a particular individual. This might be by direct observation, following a person around for an entire day. But more likely it will be through having the person write out a job description or tell you in an interview everything he or she does.

That means each part of every task the person performs. To take what many people might think is the simplest example, a receptionist's duties could include opening the mail, putting the mail on people's desks, answering the telephone, routing calls to the correct offices, taking messages, giving messages, greeting visitors to the office and announcing them or conducting them to the people they've come to see, serving coffee to visitors who have to wait (and making the coffee), typing letters and memoes, and making copies.

Then examine the list of tasks and ask a series of questions for each one:

1. What is this person doing, and how?

2. Is this task important to the efficient functioning of this business?

3. Is this the most efficient way for this task to be done?

4. Is this the best person to do this?

5. Who might better be assigned to do this?

6. Who else needs to know what this person does?

7. How often does this information need to be updated?

8. What's the best way to circulate this information?

9. What input does this person need from other employees or departments to do the job properly, or to improve present performance?

10. How might this job be better integrated into the smooth running of the rest of the company?

11. Are there other duties which could logically be assigned to this person?

12. What can the person doing the job, and those people who are directly affected by the job, suggest as changes or improvements?

Let's say that in the example of the receptionist just given, we find she delivers mail and messages by leaving her desk and visiting every office in the building. She does this after the mail comes and several times during the day as messages mount up. When visitors want coffee, she goes to the break room down the hall and fetches it for them. Whenever she's away from her desk, the office manager's secretary is supposed to back her up on answering the telephone and greeting visitors, although this secretary isn't always available.

The receptionist also has to make copies for several members of the staff, but she can't do this if the copy machine is out of toner. The office manager's secretary is in charge of office machines and supplies, but when the secretary is out of the office or taking dictation, the receptionist has to wait, which happens once or twice a week.

The receptionist herself dislikes trying to locate people to answer their phone calls. Often they aren't in their offices, and she doesn't know where to find them; yet they complain if they don't get phone calls they've been waiting for, or if they aren't notified promptly when visitors arrive for appointments.

The receptionist also gets frustrated when she has to wait for the office manager's secretary to help with the copy machine. It's the receptionist who fields the complaints from staffers whose copies are late, and who sometimes has to stay after quitting time to finish rush copying.

The office manager's secretary resents taking time away from her duties to back up the receptionist. She gets particularly annoyed when it involves trying to track down people whose appointments have arrived and bringing coffee to the visitors.

With all these facts in hand, the manager looks carefully at the list of twelve questions. A couple of days later, some changes are announced.

1. The receptionist will no longer leave the reception area except during breaks and lunch hour. A set of wooden cubbyholes is hung on the wall next to her desk, each cubbyhole labeled with the name of one employee. Each employee has a cubbyhole. All mail, messages, memoes, etc., will be placed in the appropriate cubbyholes, and workers may check them as they come in every morning and again when they return from lunch.

2. A public address system will be wired throughout the premises. When a message or visitor arrives for employees who can't be reached on their telephone extensions, the receptionist will broadcast the information on the p.a.

3. Any employee who has been away from his or her work station should buzz the receptionist on the interoffice phone line and ask if any messages have come in. The receptionist can then read the messages over the phone.

4. The receptionist will become the office manager's secretary's backup person for office supplies and machines. This means the receptionist will be trained to add toner to the copy machine when necessary, and will be authorized to order fresh supplies when she runs low.

5. A coffee machine will be installed in the reception area, from which visitors may serve themselves.

6. Since the office manager's secretary has a busy and responsible job, she will no longer be required to back up the receptionist during breaks and lunch hours. These duties will be assigned to a clerk typist from the mail room. However, the secretary will continue to provide backup during the rest of the day if the receptionist becomes unusually busy.

Now, who is notified of these changes? Everyone whose work will be affected. All those who receive mail, memoes, messages, and visitors naturally must know. The secretary and mail room clerk whose jobs will change slightly have to be told, and the clerk trained to her new duties. And, of course, anyone within sound of the p.a. — which should be everyone on the payroll — has to know what it's for.

Those workers who normally have little or nothing to do with any of the receptionist's functions can probably be notified in a memo circulated to all employees. However, those who have frequent interactions with the receptionist, which would probably mean management and administrative staff, should be told in person at a general meeting, where the new systems will be explained to them. To aid their memories, they should also be given a written list of the changes.

This is just a small example of one fairly routine job change. Once you get used to looking at these things and breaking them down, you may find yourself surprised at how easy it is to reorganize duties and responsibilities.

Sometimes it's not that simple, though. It's particularly difficult in the case of functions that involve several different parts of the company, and where large numbers of people have been doing things in a particular way for as long as they've worked there.

That's why it's important to start out with good systems, and to update them regularly. Whenever a new position is added to the company and whenever you move your business into new areas, you should look at all your old job descriptions and systems to see what needs changing. Sometimes nothing will change. More often, though, you'll find jobs that need to be split up and duties reassigned; systems that are no longer efficient; people who are doing too much; people whose talents would be put to better use if they were promoted or given more responsibility; and occasionally people you don't really need any more.

FOUR AREAS TO CONCENTRATE ON

If you think I've been putting a lot of emphasis on this business of setting up systems and organizing efficiently, remember Tom. If he'd started out setting up good systems right from the beginning, he'd probably still be in business — and his home — with his wife — today.

It's much easier to establish efficient routines from the beginning, before everyone gets caught up in the daily concerns of their jobs, and before poor organizational techniques become a habit. Remember, it's easier to form good habits than to break bad ones. And if you stress good work techniques from the start, both you and your employees will be aware of efficiency as a priority, and more alert for ways to increase it.

The first year of any new business is critical to future success. It's almost impossible to exaggerate the importance of a good start to each of the functions of your company. Since every business is unique, I can't tell you exactly what to do. I can, however, point out areas common to almost every business where you need to exercise particular care. Look at these areas to be sure you and anyone who works for you is organizing efficiently both within the department and between all other departments.

1. *Generating customer expectations.*
    This is the sales effort, and includes all advertising, public relations, professional image, interviews, packaging, sales talks — anything that increases customer awareness of you, your business, or your product.

Be sure anyone involved in this knows exactly what you're selling and who you're selling it to. They must coordinate their estimates of demand for the product and their promises of what the product will do, length of time between purchase and delivery, purchase terms, and the company's guarantees for performance or refunds, with all other employees who are concerned. This might include people in production or purchasing, quality control, order processing, inventory, warehousing, shipping, accounting, credit, customer service, and reordering.

2. *Fulfilling customer expectations.*

This is the opposite side of the previous point. It depends on all those involved making sure they meet the goals stated publicly by the sales effort.

When any problems arise between expectations and fulfillment, those on the fulfillment end should immediately notify those on the sales end. If advertising promises MasterCard credit and accounting doesn't have MasterCard privileges, accounting tells advertising immediately. When the sales force promises five-day delivery and production is ten days behind demand, production notifies the sales force. If shipping is running fifteen days behind, they'd better tell the sales force, too. Everyone involved, especially you as the owner, can contribute to the solution. It may be something as simple as hiring temporary help in the shipping department, or applying for MasterCard privileges. But whatever it is, it should be handled immediately.

Every effort should be made to fulfill the expectations created by the sales campaign. It's bad for business to tell customers they aren't going to receive what they were promised. If it's totally impossible to meet those expectations, however, revise the sales pitch. False advertising is illegal.

3. *Maintaining standards and smooth performance.*

Under this category we include all functions that keep customer relations pleasant after the initial sale, as well as those that contribute to high performance within the company.

Once a sale is made, customer service, attention to complaints, repairs, or maintenance on the customer's merchandise might be necessary. Again, items frequently brought to these departments should be noted and the details relayed to any employees who need to know.

Within the company, quality control, inventory and production, or reordering, and regular problem-solving must be regulated on an organized basis. For this to work, those in charge of these jobs must communicate with sales and ordering departments as well as customer service or repair.

4. *Cash flow, credit, and accounting.*

First, last, and always you must know how much money comes in, how much goes out, where it goes, and what it pays for. Many entrepreneurs have the idea they should keep accounting information a deep secret between themselves and their bankers. Nothing could be farther from the truth. The head of every department has to know how much the company will commit to the department's function.

When a manager has a definite budget to work with, he or she is much better able to decide whether a proposed project is too expensive, not ambitious enough, or likely to increase profits. Knowing the business can afford X dollars a month or a year for a department makes the employees more responsive to the needs of the company.

For instance, an advertising manager with a dollars-and-cents limit is better able to understand whether the company needs an advertising assistant or more television time. Employees can also help find ways to cut nonessential costs to make room in their budgets for items they feel they need more. Telling them exactly how much they have to spend gives them incentive to make these decisions wisely.

Naturally, to allocate money by department, you need a way to track which expenses are generated by each area and to project how much should be spent on each. Professional Certified Public Accountants can be hired on a short-term basis to set up these systems initially. Then once a year or so your CPA can do a review to see whether your accounting system needs changes.

When you plan to use a computer, you can often find programs already written to suit your type of business. If necessary, the company that sells your computer and the programs you use can often tailor a program to your business, or recommend a specialist to aid you.

Whatever you do, don't put off installing a clear, efficient accounting system right from the start. This is your best indicator of how healthy your business is. In addition, it gives you the figures government agencies require on tax returns and other reports. Failure to provide this information is simply not tolerated, and it must be accurate.

As you can see, starting a business is more than renting some space and hanging up a sign. Especially in the first year, you must dedicate your time and energy to making your best possible effort.

Some of the situations and problems you'll face can't be predicted ahead of time; others will turn out to be totally different than what you expected. For this reason, entrepreneurs have to be creative and flexible.

They don't have to be geniuses or even experts in everything, though. They can seek advice from others at every step of the way. And as the business grows and takes form, they can hire people to help on a long-term basis.

Finding the right people to help takes time and certain skills, though. And keeping them working for you, loyally and productively, takes some other skills. That's why I want to take the next two chapters to talk about these important aspects of running a business.

CHAPTER 9

A TEAM TO GROW ON

O ne idea I try to stress in all my books and seminars is that you don't have to become successful all by yourself. In fact, you probably can't. At some point you're going to need the help of others.

In real estate investment, you need sellers, buyers, tenants, bankers, title officers, property inspectors, brokers, and friends. You'll need the cooperation, if not active encouragement, of those who live with you, date you, or claim to love you.

You'll also need advice from books, teachers, professional contacts, those who succeeded before you, and various specialists such as attorneys and accountants.

You'll use all this help just to succeed in a business that's often regarded as a career one person manages alone. How much more help, then, can you use to build a business offering products or services to a wide customer base?

My answer to that is, all the help you can get, and all you can afford.

Luckily, this help is readily available. Visit the business section of your local library or bookstore, and you'll find shelves filled with volumes of advice, not to mention cassette tapes.

For more specialized works, try the nearest college library. You can probably arrange for borrowing privileges; but if you can't, you can read all you want while you're there. I've never seen a college library yet that required credentials from people who just want to visit.

The Yellow Pages of your telephone book list helpful services available in your area. Watch the business pages of your local newspapers for announcements of lectures and seminars. Attend meetings of business-oriented groups in your community to meet the people who can become your greatest local resources and closest friends. And subscribe to business magazines for regular articles of advice, ideas, and encouragement, as well as the ads informing you of still more learning opportunities.

At some point, though, you'll need a network of people who understand your goals and the specific company you form to reach them. When you reach that point, you'll start forming the team of individuals who can help you realize your dreams.

YOUR PERSONAL TEAM

Right here I'd like to open a subject that most business success courses ignore. If you have someone special in your life — your spouse — your boyfriend or girlfriend — your "significant other" — that person has to be part of your team. Or at least someone who won't interfere with your dreams and goals. If that isn't possible, you have an important choice to make. Which do you need and want most: the success you dream of, or that important person in your life?

There's no way I can make this decision for you. You must weigh your own priorities. Is the relationship important enough to make you give up all your hopes and dreams? Twenty or thirty years from now, when you face retirement on a meager company pension, could you say to yourself, "It's all worth it because I had Sidney all these years"?

Take a long, hard look at this. If you give up all your goals and hopes, and then this person leaves you, how will you feel? I know that's hard to think of, but force yourself. It's happened to others, and it could happen to you. Will you think, "Well, that's the way it goes, now I can start working toward those goals I set aside"? Or will you feel, "All that wasted time; if I hadn't put off my dreams for you, I could have been somebody by now"?

Only you know your relationship and your situation well enough to either get this person on your team or make a choice. If you make your own feelings clear, and explain what you want to do, and why, I think most people who truly care about you will be willing to help. If they won't help, and they won't agree at least not to interfere in what you want to do, try to listen to their objections and understand their reasoning.

This is often helpful. Perhaps the other person sees a serious flaw in your plan. Once this is pointed out to you, you can get busy remedying it.

On the other hand, the objections might come from insecurity or a lack of faith in you. Some people will be reassured if you show them the business won't come between you, or that you've taken care to protect your home and the security of your family.

There are some people, though, whom you'll never be able to convince you're doing the right thing. I really don't know what to tell you in that case. It's very difficult to face the rest of the world with confidence when those who live with you won't give you support and encouragement. At the risk of meddling in your personal affairs, I would suggest some family or marital counseling.

CHOOSING
EXPERT HELP

That's the personal side. On the business side, every entrepreneur needs at least one good attorney and one good accountant. You can find these people through referrals, through contacts you make while you're studying and learning the field, or by choosing several candidates from the phone book and interviewing them. Make sure these people understand the business you're trying to start, and have experience in helping people in your position. Ask for references from other clients they've worked with.

Your accountant and attorney should be the best you can find and afford in your area. This is not the place to cut corners with promising beginners who are willing to learn. At least some of their learning could be at your expense. Let someone else pay for the practical education of your business advisers; you hire them after they've proven themselves.

Ideally, these two people will help you lay the foundations of your company and then stay with you for years. You'll rely on their advice for the form of ownership you should use, contracts, expansions, ventures into new areas, and a host of other important decisions. If necessary, they should also be at your side in case of trouble — lawsuits, audits, reorganization, etc.

Since your relationship will be close and vital to your success, look for people you respect and can work with easily. It helps, too, if your attorney and accountant get along well and can work with each other.

In addition, you should build good relationships with at least three bankers. Make these part of your professional network, along with suppliers, distributors, and everyone you can meet who's in the same business you are, or a related line. You can get to know many of these people through local business associations, civic organizations, and attending industry meetings and conventions.

At some point in almost any successful business you'll reach the point where you hire other people to work for you. This may mean dozens or even hundreds of employees before you ever open the doors, or one or two assistants a couple of years down the road. That depends on what you're doing.

Since I can't know everyone's needs, I'm going to give you a collection of general guidelines that apply to the majority of situations. Once again, it's up to you to tailor these remarks to your needs.

WHO SHOULDN'T YOU HIRE?

I'm constantly amazed at the way some people hire employees. They'll take on a brother-in-law's cousin who's been out of a job for months, or somebody they know from their health club, and never check these people out. Or they'll hire workers on the basis of where they live, or who they worked for last.

I even know someone who — oh, no one will believe this. But it's true, I swear it. Someone I know hired a man for an executive position when his work wasn't exactly what the entrepreneur wanted. But the applicant had played a professional sport at one time. The business owner's young son had recently taken up the same sport. The boss thought maybe he could get free lessons for the boy by hiring the ex-pro. Sort of an employer's fringe benefit.

Incredible, isn't it? As it turned out, the ex-pro was good at his job, and never did supply any free lessons. By the reactions to his work, though, and the turn conversations with the boss often took, he very quickly figured out the real reason he was hired. He left as soon as he found another company that valued him for his business talents.

You hire people because you have a job that needs doing. Either the applicant is the best person you can find for the job, at the salary you're paying, or not. If not, it's not good for the business or the applicant to hire someone on the basis of other benefits you hope to get from that person.

Which also means it's not wise business judgment to hire a

person solely because you're attracted to him or her. If the most attractive applicant is also the best for the job — well, maybe. Although I'll have more to say about mixing your personal and business life later on.

This leads us to the related subject (pardon the pun) of hiring family members and good friends. Turning down your nearest and dearest when they ask for jobs is enough to make you feel like Scrooge before he met the ghosts of Christmas. But sometimes hiring them leads to even worse situations.

Naturally, you want to help out your buddies and relatives. It's fun to work with your favorite people. And let's face it, most of us enjoy that kind of power — not in any dictatorial way, but in being able to say, "What, good old Bob wants a job? Sure thing, Bob, you're on the payroll as of this minute."

Yes, that's great. You get to feel all warm and good inside, Bob thinks you're a swell guy or gal, and the two of you can have lunch together. It's a lot of fun, in the beginning.

What happens, though, when good old Bob makes mistakes? At first it may be easier to talk to him than to a stranger, if your relationship is close enough to allow criticism. But if Bob continues to mess up, your corrections can get embarrassing for both of you. There may even be times when you don't correct Bob's mistakes because you can't face calling him on the carpet again.

This is bad business practice. The time will come when you must draw problems to Bob's attention and ask him to do a better job. Eventually a certain coolness can spring up between you.

Then there's the problems that come up when good old Bob wants a raise. You may give him one when you can't really afford it, and that's no good for business. But if you don't give him one, it can affect your friendship. Then what?

Work problems may creep into your social relationship, too. You might begin avoiding each other in your hours away from work. You can excuse it by claiming you see so much of each other during working hours; the truth is more likely that working together is damaging your friendship.

The worst case is when Bob proves so inept at the job that you have to fire him. Then how will you both feel? What do you think it will do to your friendship? If you're related, how will the rest of the family react?

The only way to avoid unpleasant situations like these is to establish impersonal hiring policies and stick to them. Analyze the job to be done and decide what skills an employee needs to do them. Then don't hire anyone who doesn't meet your minimum standards. When that's a friend or relative, okay. But be careful to treat each other professionally at work.

FINDING FUTURE EMPLOYEES

Sometimes you don't need to hire your own staff right away. Consider temporaries, or letting some work out to independent contractors. Many companies have even closed whole departments and turned their work over to independents.

It's a question of costs and priorities. Do you have an ongoing need for someone and enough work to keep that person busy, either full-time or part-time, on a regular basis? Does the work require some understanding of your business? Or could it be done by anyone with some knowledge of standard practices in a certain field, whether secretarial or advertising?

Consider, too, that when you're the employer, you pay benefits and taxes for each employee. That's why some businesses prefer to hire independent contractors, who are responsible for their own taxes and benefits. However, you can't ask an independent to work only for you, and in some categories can't require them to put in specified hours at your place of business.

You can advertise for applicants, whether for staff jobs or as independent contractors, in newspapers and trade journals, or you can hire through an agency. It all depends on what you're looking for and how much interviewing you're prepared to do.

Also, before you advertise, decide exactly what you'll settle for. Are you going after the best possible person for the job, regardless of cost? Or can you get along with someone who's not so great, but doesn't command such a high salary?

Generally, when you're hiring people for important key positions, you need the best you can afford. If you want someone who's strong in an area that you don't know much about, you're going to have to pay for that expertise. When you can't pay top wages, you'll have to settle for employees with less knowledge, shorter track records, or poor employment histories.

Jobs that don't call for much specialized knowledge, those you could train almost anyone to do, go for much lower salaries. When you're only planning to pay minimum scale, expect students and older people who haven't worked much. Some of these are very good; most of them come and go like new television shows in the fall. Expect to go through about three flakes for every good person you find. When you find the good ones, give them raises and hang on to them.

Every job hunter reads the newspaper classifieds. That's probably where you'll reach the largest pool of potential employees, and also the most varied.

An ad is likely to pull applications from every skill level within a job category and usually several people who have no qualifications at all. They apply hoping you won't find anyone better or might take a chance on a trainee. You're likely to hear from an agency or two, offering to take the search off your hands. Independent contractors may also send you brochures on the benefits of using their services rather than hiring a staff position.

You can set up your ad with a phone number; an address; or a box number. It depends on how much time you want to devote to answering inquiries and how many applicants you want to see.

When you give out a phone number, interested applicants can be prescreened and the best of them given appointments for personal interviews. It's hard to tell over the phone just what someone's qualifications are, though. Also, it's easy for applicants to lie to get an interview. They figure the person answering the phone probably won't remember them later, and may not be the actual interviewer. Be prepared for someone in your office to spend a lot of time on the phone when you use this method — and have that person take notes on every call.

Your ad can request resumes, to be sent to an address or box number. When you give your street address, a few eager applicants are apt to hand deliver their resumes. Usually these people can be diverted by the secretary or receptionist. She simply tells them she'll pass the resume along and someone will call them to make an appointment later if they qualify.

Of course, this still wastes the time of someone in your office. And if you don't have a secretary or receptionist yet, it will interrupt you or whoever is nearest the door.

The address could be given with a particular time for applicants to come in. Then you make yourself available to whoever shows up during those hours. In those cases, you have to be sure you're there when you said you would be. This also leaves you open to occasional interruptions from people who can't come during the specified hours.

A box number allows you to sort through applications with little chance of being interrupted by eager job seekers. You then contact only those who look like the best candidates.

Of course, you can allow an agency to do your prescreening. (When you're looking for skilled administrators, these are called executive placement counselors, executive recruitment services, or headhunters.) Simply tell the agency exactly what you require. Ideally, they'll send you people who meet your standards. They'll often give employment tests in advance, and tell you the scores for each applicant.

It takes a little time to work out a good relationship with an agency. Their counselors usually get paid on a commission basis. Either you or the applicant you hire pays a percentage of the new employee's salary to the agency. This system makes employment counselors very eager to place people, since they don't earn any money unless you hire one of their clients.

Different agents react to this in different ways. Some try to build a solid reputation of only sending out the best qualified people for each job. They take pride in having their first or second candidate hired and declared a perfect match. These agents usually work with a solid list of satisfied companies who call them again and again.

Others, unfortunately, take the opposite approach. They send out anybody they have on their client lists, then call the interviewer and do a hard sell. They'll lie about clients' test scores and encourage applicants to falsify their backgrounds. Since the applicants' backgrounds were supposedly verified by the agency, few companies bother to screen them again.

When you consider using an agency, check around among other businesspeople. Find out which agents have the best reputations and which are untrustworthy. Sometimes, of course, you can end up with the only poor agent at an otherwise good agency. Occasionally, too, an agency will change hands and technique. But when you find a dependable agency, the time and trouble it saves you can be worth any fees you might pay.

How about agencies where the applicant pays the fee? It depends on what you want. Normally, the most qualified people for a job don't pay their own fees. Those who do pay are usually the ones with little experience or poor skills. This may not be true all the time in every part of the country and for every job category, though. In a depressed job market, even the best workers may be willing to pay someone to find them employment.

Finally, you can advertise in trade journals or industry newsletters. You do this when you're looking for skill and experience in a specialized line of work.

Sorting Your Prospects

Once you attract a pile of applications, what do you do? First, naturally, you look for people who meet the minimum requirements you set up for the job. Next, examine their employment histories. Someone who's held seventeen jobs in the last five years may not stay long with you.

You'll probably end up with a large pile of discards, a smaller pile of good prospects, and a few maybes. Set up personal interviews with your best applicants first, since you want to save as much time as possible. Remember, no matter how much you enjoy meeting new people, your time is valuable.

When interviewing, try to set the applicant at ease as quickly as possible. Get him or her to talk. The more information you have, the better you'll be able to decide whether you want to work with this person.

Unless you've absolutely decided to hire a candidate, end the interview on a friendly but noncommittal note. Stand up, move toward the door, and say something like, "Thank you for coming in.

We'll be calling the applicant we choose on Friday afternoon."

Setting a time frame and stating you'll call only the chosen person then will save you from having to call every unsuccessful applicant. It also lets the applicants know that if they don't hear from you by that time, they'd better keep looking elsewhere.

As soon as each applicant leaves, jot down some notes on the back of the application or resume, or on a separate page you clip to the application. Make sure you describe your reactions well enough to jog your memeory after you've seen several people in a row.

If you've already decided not to hire someone, state a reason. Remember, though, that you can't discriminate because of age, race or ethnic background, sex, physical handicaps, marital status, or family status, unless one of these has actual bearing on the job. For instance, you can eliminate someone over forty if you need a teenage fashion model. But you can't set up a work requirement that really has nothing to do with the job and then use it to avoid hiring certain classes of people.

One example of this that comes to mind is a company that required all its warehouse workers to be able to lift and carry eighty pounds. Eventually a woman sued, claiming this wasn't a true job requirement. She said the company used it as an excuse not to hire women.

During the subsequent court case it came out that nothing in the warehouse weighed over about twenty pounds. Dollies and wheeled carts were provided for moving items in groups, so even carrying a dozen pieces was no problem. And any healthy woman is able to lift and move items weighing twenty pounds or less — just ask the mother of any two-year-old.

The woman won her case. The company was ordered to give her a job and pay her back pay from the date she was first refused work, plus extra compensation for discrimination.

It's not worth it to discriminate. However, if you're going to be working closely with someone, you are allowed to refuse applicants on grounds of personal preference. A reason such as "Acts like a know-it-all. He'd drive me crazy in two weeks," or "Fidgets and giggles like a teenager, she makes me nervous just watching her," is acceptable, as long as it's true.

BE SURE
WHO YOU HIRE

When you think you've found the best candidate for the job, you still have some checking to do. Certain individuals prepare great background descriptions for themselves and come across impressively at interviews. The only problem is, they aren't as good as they appear on the surface.

Contact previous employers, tell them you're thinking of hiring this person, and ask for information. Be sure to ask what the person did for them and if the work was satisfactory. Inquire why the person left. Then comes what may be the most revealing question of all: Would you hire this person to work for you again?

Some employers won't give out information over the telephone. In those cases, simply ask your questions in a letter, leaving room for answers.

Occasionally a job-seeker will ask you not to contact a current employer. This is fair. Some employers will purposely give a poor reference to avoid losing a valuable worker. Others fire employees who seek new jobs.

While your sympathies may be with the boss who's about to lose an employee, remember that the only way many people can move up is to move over. Workers have a right to look for better conditions, higher salaries, and more responsibility. That's the way business works, and you might as well accept it, even though some day you'll probably be the boss who gets left. When it happens, wish your employees well and give them fair references. Make them part of your outside network. They may steer some new business your way if you stay on good terms with them.

Merely checking references may not be enough when employees will be trusted with something of value. Those who handle or travel with money or valuable merchandise, who have access to company secrets, or who often work alone may need to be checked more closely. A professional bonding agency will investigate for police records and insure you against employee theft of money or goods.

When you need more complete knowledge of an applicant's background, hire a private detective agency. This is often done in highly competitive industries such as electronics, where inside knowledge of a competitor's new products can be worth millions of dollars. You may want to know if someone has ties to or contacts in other companies before you reveal company secrets.

PROTECT YOURSELF

If your business does rely on information or processes that aren't known to similar companies, you'll need to take some other measures to protect yourself as well. In the information industries, copyrights are used to establish rights to books, tapes, videos, and motion pictures.

When you put a lot of work and money into developing an image around a company or product name, or a logo, you don't want someone else profiting from that identity. Protect names and logos through trademark registration.

Inventions and processes are a different matter. The patent office exists to register these types of new ideas. Theoretically, once you register a patent, you have the exclusive right to your idea for a number of years: seventeen, fourteen, seven, or three, depending on what you patent.

However, patent files are open to the public. Many people go through them expressly to find ideas which can be changed slightly and still work without violating the patent. Hundreds of inventors regret they ever filed patents on their work. Certainly, once a good idea comes on the market, people are going to copy it as closely as they can. But there's no sense letting them start before you're ready to sell your model.

Don't get me wrong; I'm not saying you should never bother with patents. But talk to a good patent attorney, one who can tell you whether your idea should be protected in advance.

All this may seem far afield from checking out employees. But it all ties together. Employee leaks can allow competitors to learn your secrets almost before you know them yourself.

In some cases, employees have actually come up with an idea while on one payroll, then sold it to the highest bidder without ever telling their employer about it. Six months later the company's chief rival brings out "their" new product and the betrayed boss wonders, "Why didn't we come up with that?"

There is no absolute guarantee this will never happen to you. You can do a couple of things to make it less likely, though. All employees in key positions to learn important company secrets should sign a nondisclosure agreement. This is a sworn statement that they will not reveal details of your inventions or processes to anyone from outside the company. You can also require them not to tell anyone inside the company who isn't cleared by you to receive the information. Your attorney can draw this up, and write in some penalties for failure to abide by the agreement.

Don't forget, too, that not only production and creative personnel have access to secrets. Secretaries often attend meetings where these subjects are discussed. In addition to secretaries, file clerks and company messengers and mail handlers often handle sensitive documents.

Another possibility for leaks occurs when key personnel leave you. When security is an issue, never allow someone leaving to clean out a desk or files. If you're firing, give the termination notice on Friday afternoon. Then you or someone else go back to the work station and watch while the person picks up personal items. Escort him or her out the door, and make sure that person never gets past the reception desk again.

It's a little more difficult when the employee quits. In that case, you should immediately ask for an inventory of sensitive material. Check the inventory carefully, looking for items that should be on it but aren't. Then check the inventory against material left in the office during the employee's last day, immediately before he or she leaves. This doesn't ensure the employee hasn't already sneaked copies out of the office. But if he or she were going to do that, it was probably already done before the person gave notice.

One last thing you can do is ask an employee to sign a noncompetition agreement. This is a statement that the person will not work for an organization or start a business that's in direct competition with you for a certain length of time. These have to be worded very carefully, and aren't always binding in some fields, so speak to your attorney about it.

Now you've got some idea how to hire people and protect yourself from them. Next, let's go into how you manage them once they're actually working for you.

CHAPTER 10

MANAGING YOUR TEAM

A s I said earlier in this book, some parts of starting and running your business will be handled simultaneously. Building and managing a staff overlap in this way, although not entirely.

When you interview and hire people, think about how and where they'll fit in, how well you'll work together, and how to motivate them to their best efforts. Once you've assembled what you think is a pretty good team, you'll do more actual managing. All the while, though, you should continue to think about ways to build and improve the staff you have.

Ideally, you'll have these thoughts in mind even as you interview your first potential employee. Since I have no idea whether you'll need assembly workers or choreographers, clerk typists or corporate lawyers, sales reps or engineers, I can't tell you exactly the types of people to hire. Again, I can only give you the general outlines to follow.

One of the primary things you'll notice as you interview is that different people have varied skills and experience. For some of them, the job you're offering will be a step up; for others it will be repetition of a job they did somewhere else; and for a few it will be a step or two down.

Personnel specialists have theories about who to choose in cases like these. I say, you can't go by theories. You have to judge each case on individual merit and how it fits into your business.

For instance, let's say you're looking for a personal assistant. You have three good applicants. Al has never done all the things you need, but is eager, willing to learn, and excited about the opportunity to grow. Bill was personal assistant to a competitor who went out of business, and he knows everything you need right now. Cathy ran an entire division of a large corporation and could manage a much bigger company than yours; she knows more about the business than you do.

Which one would you hire?

Personnel theory says choose Bill. He's proved he can handle the job, will take a minimum of your time to train, and will take the greatest load off you immediately. Al is unproven, and needs training. Cathy is overqualified; her ability is so much greater than the job requires that she may get bored and leave before you can take advantage of all the extra knowledge she brings with her.

THEORIES CAN BE WRONG FOR YOU

I say, look at the person, the job, and the future of the company.

Maybe Al makes up for something you lack. He could be a detail person, who'll take the boring chores off your hands while you concentrate on more interesting matters. Also, his lack of training could mean he'll work for a lower salary. If he won't be in sole charge of a key position, such as marketing, Al may be what you need.

Bill, with all his experience, might not actually be best. If he's done the same job before, and wants to do it again, he could lack ambition. When the position calls for someone willing to grow, someone flexible enough to change as the job demands, Bill may not be able to handle it.

Also, if he worked for a competitor who failed, Bill could have had some bad business habits trained into him on that last job. Can you identify any such problems and train him out of them? Of course, if you want someone who'll do the job right now, and keep doing it for years, Bill's probably your man.

Yes, Cathy's overqualified — at present. Ask her straight out why she's willing to take such a long step down. She could be fed up with being an anonymous cog in a huge machine, or with corporate politics. Maybe she longs for a small company where she really makes a difference, or the excitement of helping build something from next to nothing.

When you have big plans for rapid growth, her expertise could be invaluable. Even if she doesn't stay long, what you learn from her could be worth it. You can always ask her to sign a contract to stay with you for six months or a year. If she's ready to leave at the end of that time, find another Al or Bill.

Do you see what I mean here? Don't just look at how well the person suits the job you need done right now. Also consider how the applicant's abilities fit into your financial picture and your future plans for the business.

Some entrepreneurs get into trouble here. They look for someone who's perfect for the present position and never consider the future. The job may grow, and you'll need someone capable of growing with it. Or, the job could stay exactly the same forever. In that case, look for someone who doesn't have a lot of ambition.

It's probably impossible to find the perfect fit between job and applicant by analyzing everything when you first hire. I really believe it's more a matter of luck and intangibles when you put the right person into the right slot and everything works smoothly. You may have to fill the same job several times before you find the best person for it.

MIX PEOPLE CAREFULLY

When you hire a single employee to work with you alone, you'll naturally look for someone you like and feel you can get along with. Once you add more people, you come up against the problem of mixing several different personalities. The more important the positions involved, the more crucial this is.

In hiring general labor — the jobs a lot of people can do with little or no training — personality mix is slightly important, but not vital. You'll naturally check with former employers to weed out serious troublemakers. If security is a consideration, you'll do an extensive background check. A few problem employees may slip into your company anyway, but replacing them isn't much trouble.

Putting together an executive staff, though, is more involved. These people must work well with you, with their counterparts in other departments — remember what I said about communication and coordination in the last chapter — and also be competent in important positions.

One way to handle this is to draw existing members of your executive staff into the decision process. When you have candidates you believe are good for the job, ask the opinion of those who will work with them. Circulate their resumes, invite them to lunch with your existing staff, ask one or two people whose judgment you trust to sit in on a briefing or interview.

GOOD PEOPLE AREN'T PERFECT

As you assemble key staff members, there's one tendency you have to beware of. Entrepreneurs are action-oriented idea people. The same qualities in others are very attractive to us. Which would you rather attend: a conference on new ways to profit over the next decade, or a meeting to discuss alphabetical versus numerical filing systems?

If you chose filing systems, you may be reading the wrong book. Unless, of course, you make money setting up files for other companies.

The point I want to make is that as entrepreneurs, we may be most attracted to the job applicant, or staff member, who comes up with fresh ideas. Within reason, that's fine. But we have to watch out for the idea person who isn't right for the job we need done.

You see, idea people aren't necessarily good managers. If we're looking for someone to manage an office, a department, or a division, we have to concentrate on hiring someone who has solid management skills.

This is most finely balanced in a small company. If each key department consists of one person — say, marketing, production, customer service, and accounting — each of these people has to wear two hats. Each one must be able to come up with ideas on how to run the department more efficiently, how to increase profits, and how to work together more effectively. At the same time, these people also must schedule their work, meet deadlines imposed by other segments of the company, respond to requests and complaints, and plan their future projects.

That means you can't hire anyone for these posts who's excellent at management but never has fresh ideas. On the other hand, neither can you hire terrific idea people who are unable to manage.

What you're most likely to get here is an uneasy compromise. The people whose ideas really excite you, but who can't manage themselves or their jobs, are no good to you. But those who always meet their deadlines while never contributing innovations aren't as valuable as they should be, either.

As a general rule, I'd say accounting and customer service have to be the most dependable functions in a company. For these positions, you can get along with good managers who don't come up with many new ideas.

Production talents depend on your business. Either management or innovation might be more important; only you can judge.

Sales and marketing have to be more creative. These people must come up with new ways to attract attention, change their techniques as the market and the economy shift, and think of new ways to meet consumer demands. However, these abilities are no use if your sales and marketing people don't launch their campaigns in time to take advantage of the best sales seasons or to meet competition.

This means you can't always get the best possible person for each department. Someone with exciting sales ideas who can't meet deadlines won't work for you. A production manager who's always on schedule but can't think of ways to cut costs or speed up manufacture may not be right, either. You'll have to take the best combination of talents, not the applicant who's strong in one important area but weak in another.

BALANCE SKILLS AND AUTHORITY

When your company's large enough, you can afford to have some of each personality type in every department. The creative people come up with fresh ideas, and the management types see that details and schedules are taken care of. The only question is, which one do you give the most authority?

Again, I'm going to have to say, it depends. Which is most important to the department and the company in general? Which can you live with yourself?

Some owners get nervous if too many employees come up with independent ideas and have the authority to implement them. Also, some creative people get so enthusiastic over new projects, they pull co-workers off necessary routine jobs to work on the fresh idea.

On the other hand, some management types are so cautious, they don't move quickly enough into untried projects. They have the attitude that after the routine is taken care of, they'll see if they have people and resources left to allocate to the new idea. Unfortunately, sometimes there aren't any "leftovers"; and when there are, they aren't always sufficient to handle the job. This frustrates the creative innovators, who feel they aren't given the support they need. When their frustration becomes too great, they leave for a job where they believe their originality will be more appreciated.

Whether you put an innovator or a manager in the top position of a department, there's bound to be some friction between the two types. But you need them both if your company is to prosper. Therefore, part of your job as a manager will be to keep relations between the two running as smoothly as possible.

CONTROLLED DELEGATION

My personal preference, in most cases, is to have a creative person in the number one spot, and a detail-oriented type as number two. Then the owner, or the owner's delegate, such as a vice president, chief executive officer, or whatever fits your structure, works very closely with all the number ones.

Every new plan is gone into in depth. Requirements in the way of budget, personnel, space, equipment, time, and whatever else might be needed are analyzed carefully. Allocations are made so the new project interferes as little as possible with any important functions or ongoing work of the department.

The new project's impact on other departments has to be looked at also. For example, an idea for a fresh product means you'll need advertising to launch it. Accounting may have to work out systems for paying and charging a new group of suppliers and customers. Or a new marketing scheme could involve accounting, customer service, and shipping departments. In each case, all departments involved have to allocate resources and set up systems with minimum interference to their other tasks.

As manager, you're responsible for seeing all this goes as smoothly as possible. Let your staff have all the input they need; then you decide what gets done. Set up schedules for each department to report back on their progress, or lack of it. Help everyone solve any problems that arise.

Remember, too, that many people, especially unambitious ones in lower level jobs, resist change. They'll pick holes in a plan, criticize it, and explain all the reasons it can't work, rather than figure how to make it work. Listen to them, up to a point. Sometimes they're right.

When they're wrong, these critics at least serve a purpose. They help you clarify your reasons for wanting to do something. Then it's your job to motivate them into putting their best efforts into the work.

MOTIVATING YOUR TEAM

A lot has been said and written about motivation in the last hundred years. It's one of the most important factors in successfully managing employees, and I'd advise you to learn as much about it as you can.

One of the most famous studies in labor motivation took place at Westinghouse back in the 1930s. A group was put to work in a room where experimenters gradually changed the lighting. They found that as they slowly, over a period of several days, made the lights brighter or dimmer, production increased.

The trouble was, production went up when the lights were changed in either direction. This blew a hole in the test scientists thought they were running, to see how much light motivated the workers to greater activity. The experimenters rechecked their tests and the reactions of the people working in the room, and found they'd stumbled on something unexpected.

Production went up because of the attention the experimenters gave to the workers.

The people working in that test room demonstrated a basic desire common to everyone. We all want attention and recognition. It's a desire so strong, most psychologists classify it as a need.

Newborn babies die if no one cuddles them and talks to them during their first months of life. Have you ever been around young children? They tug at parents' hands, legs, and clothes for attention.

As they get a little older, they call, "Look at me! Mama, Daddy, look at me!" Teenagers act boisterous and wear outrageous styles to attract notice.

Do you think adults outgrow this need for attention and recognition? Dale Carnegie, the famous speaker, wrote a book called *How to Win Friends and Influence People*. In that book he advises readers to call new acquaintances by name at least three times during their initial conversation, because a person's own name is the most important sound in the world to its owner. If you use it, you recognize the person as an individual and demonstrate your attention to him or her. The person you're talking to will remember you more warmly for it.

Why do you think most people like expensive homes, fancy cars, nice clothes, gold and precious gems, and all the latest status symbols? Yes, these things make life more comfortable, they look good, they're fun to own. But just as importantly, they bring us admiration from others. Our parents, friends, and even total strangers can see at a glance how successful we are and what good taste we have.

This even works in reverse. Some groups give recognition to members who ignore current styles and don't value symbols of success. The less ambitious an individual is, the less regard he or she has for status symbols, the more other members of the group admire and try to copy or outdo that person.

People like to be noticed. Given a choice, most of us prefer to be noticed favorably — complimented, praised for achievements, told what great guys and gals we are. But if we can't get that, we'll go the other way.

Every parent and grammar school teacher knows children sometimes misbehave to get attention. Police officers can tell you of crimes committed simply to get recognition for the criminal. Sadder still are their stories about innocent people who confess to unsolved murders. Those who surrender for crimes they don't commit are almost always introverted, lonely individuals who want sómeone to notice them.

By now, you should realize this is one of the greatest tools you have for motivating employees and gaining their loyalty. As the boss, you're going to be one óf the most important people in their lives. Use this advantage wisely, and your staff will work miracles for you.

Along with this, one of the best pieces of management advice I ever got came from a source I can't even remember now. It went, "Praise publicly, criticize in private."

Compliment your employees. Find nice things you can say — sincerely, because everyone who works for you will soon know when you mean it and when you don't. Then say those nice things in front of as many people as possible.

You don't have to spend your entire day running around finding one good thing to say about everyone who works for you. If you have a large company, or one with branches in several locations, that isn't even possible.

CREATIVE RECOGNITION

Use your imagination. As you come into a meeting with your executive staff, say things like, "Good morning, Fred. I got your report on why sales were down last quarter, and it looks like you put a lot of hard work into it. I'd like to talk to you about it when I've had time to give it the attention it deserves."

That's lots better than saying something like, "That was an awfully long report you wrote, Fred. I haven't had time to wade through it all, but I'll get back to you eventually."

Do you see the subtle difference between the two versions of the same message? The first one acknowledges Fred's effort. You say you value his work so much that you want to give it special attention. The second statement implies you wish he hadn't done so much, and sounds as though you resent having to review his report.

Later in the same meeting, you might pick out another of your executives to compliment. At the next meeting, praise two other people.

Once or twice a week say something to those you see regularly. Thank your secretary for retyping a letter. Tell the receptionist you appreciate the way she handles your messages. Compliment your attorney on the extra work she put in analyzing your new business plan.

It doesn't matter too much what you notice, as long as you're sincere and communicate that you see and appreciate those around you. When your company is too large for you to communicate personally with every worker, get your managers and supervisors into the act as well.

Set up incentive programs. These can be along the lines of most productive workers of the week or the month, most compliments from customers, best design, or whatever's appropriate for your business.

Don't keep the results of these little contests a secret between the worker and the supervisor. Announce them at a full meeting of the entire branch or department. Print the names in the company newsletter.

Make sure each supervisor passes details of accomplishments to your secretary. Then send a personal letter to everyone who's achieved something worthwhile. These letters don't have to be long and flowery. Just say something simple like:

> Dear Max:
>
> I'm impressed with the way you've rearranged the warehouse to fill orders more efficiently. People like you make United Widget the fastest growing newcomer in our industry. Thank you for doing your job so well.
>
> Sincerely,
> Betty Boss

Let your secretary make up the letters herself, and then compliment her on the warm way she handles them. But don't use form letters; that would take away the personal touch you're after. Send a carbon copy to Max's supervisor, to be posted on the department bulletin board where everyone can see how much the boss appreciates Max.

That should give you some ideas for the "praise publicly" part of my advice. Now, what about the "criticize in private" portion?

CAREFUL CRITICISM

Some bosses seem to think people only work hard if they're frightened. They chew out employees in front of co-workers, embarrass them in front of visitors, and call meetings to announce mistakes. This may work, sometimes, for some people. However, it usually works against you in the long run.

The one or two out of a hundred employees who work better under these conditions may respond, at least temporarily. But even most of them eventually decide they've had enough and quit. Meanwhile, what's happening to the rest of your staff?

The large majority of people dislike working for someone with a short temper and a sharp tongue. Even if they're never the objects of your wrath, they'll worry that someday their turn will come. And while they may feel the person you reprimand had it coming, they'll still be uncomfortable at witnessing a public dressing down.

Morale slips under these conditions. Efficiency goes down as employees start thinking of you as a "rough boss." Many of those with opportunities will leave you, and the ones who can't will resent you. They'll criticize you behind your back, and be reluctant to draw problems to your attention for fear of attracting blame.

When your staff won't tell you about problems, business suffers. Small hitches you might have corrected easily in the beginning can grow to giant proportions before you find out about them. By that time, it may be too late to do anything.

Therefore, when you have to correct an employee, do it in a private meeting. And don't let the whole meeting be an unrelieved criticism session. That can sap a good worker's energy for days or even weeks.

Instead, start out with some praise. Then slip in a short discussion of the major problem. Be specific, but impersonal. Ask the employee why the problem exists and whether he or she can think of a solution. Set schedules for solving problems or reviewing progress. When you've aired that, add a few more compliments.

After all, you hired this person, and he or she must have some assets to stay on the payroll. Mention them.

This technique enables the employee to feel good after criticism. You don't want someone going back to work thinking, "Jeez, I never do anything right, what's the point of trying?" or "That old grouch, always on somebody's back, nothing's ever good enough, so why try?"

You want your workers to leave your office thinking, "That Pete's sure a nice guy to work for. Now that he's pointed it out, I know exactly how to do a better job. Can't wait to get started — wouldn't want to let him down!"

If you want people to do their best work for you, make them feel good about themselves and about their jobs. Do this by showing them you recognize and value them as people, and you appreciate their contributions to the success of your business.

After all, you really are all on the same team. A friendly team works better together than one where hostilities and resentment boil under the surface — and occasionally let off steam. So treat your employees in a friendly, respectful manner, not like naughty children or stubborn idiots.

BE FRIENDLY FROM A DISTANCE

By friendly and respectful, though, I don't mean you must become close friends with your employees. That leads to the sort of problems I mentioned in the last chapter. In addition, it can create tensions in your workplace.

I know most people make friends at work. This is especially true for entrepreneurs who spend most of their waking hours at work during the early years of starting a business. Everyone needs some human companionship, and it's normal to look for it from the people you see most.

However, it's very rare for a boss to keep and maintain close friendships with those who work for him or her. I'm not saying it's impossible, but it is extremely difficult.

For one thing, it is impossible to like everyone who works with you exactly the same amount. Human nature being what it is, those workers who feel you favor a co-worker's company over theirs are apt to feel jealous. This may come out in subtle ways — neglecting requests from your friend, or being a little slow or sloppy in doing the work.

On the other hand, opportunists in the company are likely to try to get closer to your friend. They figure being close to your friend is the next best thing to being close to the boss. This may cause them to put extra effort into work for your friend while neglecting other necessary tasks.

And then we come full circle to those who are jealous of your friend. They resent the way others ignore them to cater to your friend. The next thing you know, you may have unexplainable slowdowns and errors without understanding why.

Your own reactions enter into this, too. You may favor suggestions from your friend, promote him or her, or otherwise show what others feel is preference. Never mind that your friend may actually deserve and have earned better treatment; some people are always going to believe he or she succeeds solely on the strength of the relationship between the two of you.

Of course, you can try to counter this by going out of your way to avoid favoritism. The danger here is that you'll offend, and possibly lose, your friend. And if that person truly is more competent and has better ideas than others on your staff, it's really not fair to hold him or her back just to avoid jealousy.

And if the two of you are of different sexes, you're really asking for the gossip to fly.

Make your friends among other entrepreneurs. It's less likely to damage your business, and you have more in common with them.

Show friendship in scrupulously fair ways to those who work for you. Have lunch or dinner with each executive in turn. Entertain everyone at a company party from time to time. If you must golf with one, then invite another to the country club to swim, offer a third the use of the tennis court, and ask the fourth to make up a theater party with you. As they say in the Army, socialize with the lower ranks, but don't fraternize.

The people who work for and with you are the foundation of your business. When you choose them carefully and manage them wisely, you build a strong basis for growth and expansion. Before you take advantage of those opportunities, though, you should be acquainted with the facts in the next chapter.

CHAPTER 11

CONTROLLING
GROWTH

I call this chapter "Controlling Growth" because control is one of the most important factors in successful expansion. Many, many entrepreneurs start profitable businesses and do well for several years. It's only when their companies start growing too quickly, without controls, that they fail.

There are several kinds of growth, depending on how your business starts and where you want to go with it. You may own one store or office in your home town and decide to double its size, or open branches in surrounding towns. You might manufacture a product sold across the United States and want to expand into overseas markets. Your company could dominate its market in one state or geographical area and be ready to go nationwide. Or you could be successful in a particular line and want to diversify into other products or services.

Whatever your base and however high you aim, though, there are certain steps you must take, both to protect your original base and to increase your chances of expanding successfully.

Your first step, of course, is to establish an initially successful business. You must be making a profit with your original venture before you consider growth.

GROWTH COSTS MONEY

This might seem self-evident to some of you, but I'm afraid it's not that clear to everyone. For some reason many entrepreneurs have the idea the solution for a business that loses money is to increase its size. Their reasoning runs along these lines: My company brings in $250,000 a year and doesn't quite break even. If we double our volume, we'll bring in $500,000 a year and make a profit.

It doesn't work that way. When people think like this, they overlook the fact that doubling the business may mean triple the work and costs for the first year or two. True, some of your marketing origination costs may be reduced. The same advertising can be used for your other branches with only slight changes. Or you can mention new products along with the old one.

However, the real key to expansion is reaching more potential customers. That means the cost of television or radio time, newspaper or magazine space, and printing and postage for flyers and catalogs rises as you place more or larger ads.

In addition, the workload increases. You have to increase production, inventory, and/or services to meet the greater demand generated by your expansion. More orders have to be filled. Paperwork escalates. You and/or your executive staff have to hire, train, and supervise more people.

Your new employees need salaries and benefits, workspace and equipment, heat, air conditioning, lights, telephones, bathrooms, etc., etc. In most cases these overhead costs must be paid before you receive the extra income you hope to generate through your expansion.

Growth strains every position and system in your company. It's a little like weightlifting. When you're prepared, you can lift in the world class, and you have as much chance at a medal as anyone. But if you pick up more than you're ready for, something will give way and knock you out of the competition. Damages can even be extensive enough to prevent you from ever competing again. So prepare yourself carefully.

When you keep thinking just a little more income will make your company profitable, look first at refining your existing systems. Maybe your present advertising could be better. Perhaps you could economize on overhead — move to cheaper quarters, eliminate one or two staff positions, cut down on electricity use, or production waste, or overtime demands. Improve customer service to build up repeat business.

Look closely at your product. Is it the best quality for the lowest price possible? Could it be improved, updated, redesigned? Go over every facet of your business looking for ways to make it profitable as it is now.

IS GROWTH REALLY WHAT YOU WANT?

When your company is making money, even if only a little, think carefully before you assume expansion is what you want. It seems to be an American custom to think "Bigger is better," but that isn't always true.

To give you an example I know well, let's take the seminar business. In the early 1980s, a lot of people were giving small real estate seminars around our home states. A few of us decided to expand our audiences with national speaking tours and television presentations.

The next thing you know, it seemed as though everyone with a real estate license was speaking all over the country and appearing on TV. All these speakers saw others going nationwide and decided growth was the only goal to aim for.

What happened next was sad, but inevitable. Many of these speakers lacked a sound financial base to support national tours. Their seminars hadn't been profitable before; the additional costs of travel, hotel bills, shipping, and support systems for nationwide personal and TV appearances was more than they could afford. Some went bankrupt, while others found they didn't enjoy the fast pace and stress of so much work, and retired.

At one point when everyone with any experience wanted a national seminar tour, I talked with a man from my home state who had a different idea. Del had been giving his seminar for several years. He had a regular circuit of cities he visited up and down the west coast from January to June. Del's philosophy went something like this:

> I work six months of the year and take the other six off. The business I generate during the six months I speak brings in enough income to support my family comfortably and put away savings for retirement. My wife and I can handle everything that needs to be done with the help of one secretary, who's been with us for twenty years and knows the business as well as we do. Why should I take on a nationwide tour? I'd have to work all year round, hire and train more people, spend more on advertising, and devote more time to supervising what goes on in the office. I couldn't enjoy my boat, or the long trips my family takes — a couple of months in France last year, and we're planning to spend next fall in Japan. I've got   exactly what I want right now. Why work myself to death to earn a lot of money I won't have time to enjoy, or run the risk of losing it all?

You could say Del lacked ambition, or was afraid to take on a new challenge. It depends on your point of view. Personally, I think Del had his priorities straight. He'd decided what he wanted for himself, and he had it. He wasn't persuaded to give up his own achievement and take on the goals others thought he should pursue just because they did.

By way of contrast, listen to the story I heard from a woman we'll call Tammy, whose husband did decide on a large expansion:

> I wish Chuck had been happy with the small business we had before. He worked short hours a few days a week, and so did I. We had a comfortable house with a swimming pool,

and a vacation home at the beach. We took most of the summer off, and several weeks during the winter. Chuck coached Little League in the spring, and I had time for lunches and shopping with my friends, and kept the house just the way I liked it. The few people who worked for us, most of them part-time, were like family. They'd all been with us from the start, and everyone got along well.

Then we got involved in this nationwide campaign. To help finance it, Chuck took in a partner. One of the terms the partner insisted on was that Chuck continue to manage the business personally, since it was his ownership that made us successful in the beginning. We thought this was going to really put us in the big time. We'd make more money than we ever dreamed of, and could retire in a few years.

Instead, it's been a disaster. For three years now, ever since Chuck decided to expand, we've both worked ten and twelve hours a day. We've had to hire a large full-time staff, and some of them act like we're trying to take advantage of them if we ask them to do one extra thing, or stay a few minutes late. They argue among themselves and play politics with Chuck and me.

We've had to give up our long vacations, because the business can't seem to get along without us for any extended period. Then we sold the beach house, since we weren't using it anyway, and the expansion cost more than we thought it would. Chuck not only gave up Little League coaching, he wasn't even able to see any of the games last season. And I had to hire a housekeeper — five of them, in fact. We can't find one who cleans to suit us, one was totally undependable, one used to lock the kids outside while she entertained her boyfriend, and one stole from us. The pool? We don't have time to clean it, let alone enjoy it.

The worst part of it is, we aren't making any more net profit than we were three years ago. Oh, the gross is five times more. But by the time we pay the bigger overhead and give the partner his share, Chuck and I take home exactly what we used to. We haven't even had a cost of living raise for inflation. We both wish we'd stayed small and happy, instead of going through all this and ending up worse off than we were before.

I'm not saying you should never expand your company. I told you about Del, and about Tammy and Chuck, because I want you to think long and hard about your goals. You can earn a comfortable living and enjoy being your own boss with a fairly small business.

Some people want more. They want much larger financial returns — large enough so they can retire early as millionaires.

Others enjoy the challenges of growth. They become bored at doing the same things day after day, no matter how successfully. They see business as the most exciting game they know, and play to win it all. Even if they lose, they'll bounce back with a new game, because they love the excitement and the feeling of achievement they get from new beginnings and rapid expansion.

So in addition to knowing your business, you must know yourself. What do you want most of all: independent comfort, or exciting new challenges?

Prepare For Growth

When your answer includes business growth, you've got some careful studying to do before you make a move. Naturally, you should know your original business inside out — what works and what doesn't, and why. Learn what your competition has tried and succeeded with; more importantly, find out where they failed, and the reasons. Ask yourself what different approach might have changed the results of failures.

Now, before you do anything else, is the time for a careful market survey. Find out whether enough demand exists to support the move you want to make. It's worth it to pay a professional firm to handle this for you, since the cost of failure is much higher than the price of an excellent survey.

Next, decide well in advance when you want to make your expansion move. For this, you'll need to be well-acquainted with all the seasonal details of your business. Most likely you'll want to start during a slack period, so that your new facilities or services are ready to take advantage of peak earning periods.

At this point, you're ready to repeat all the moves that went into opening your original venture. You have a big advantage this time around, since you've gained so much experience. However, don't become over-confident and neglect any important details.

Make a careful analysis of your current cash flow. Then project all the factors that will go into your expansion plan. Your new venture may not break even for almost as long as it took to show a profit with your original company. Can you afford the drain on your assets for that long?

If not, you'll have to look for outside money. This may come from loans and credit; now is the time to increase your line of credit and look for new ones with other financial institutions. It's hardest to get money when you need it worst, so prepare for this in advance.

Predict as closely as possible how you plan to change your marketing approach to reach a wider audience. Will you continue to advertise in the same way, only on a larger scale? Or should you try new methods and media?

Then look at your production and distribution capacity. It's no use to create greater demand if you can't fulfill it. You may have to add to your manufacturing capability, increase inventory, or do more shipping.

When you're examining these departments, consider whether to increase the size of your central location or to diversify into new geographical locations. Keeping everything in one place simplifies control and makes it easier to train new workers, since all your experienced people are together. On the other hand, several smaller facilities could make more sense.

For one thing, it's usually easier to find smaller physical plants. For another, shipping and distribution are normally faster and cheaper over short distances. Even if your business consists of retail stores, which naturally are separated by some distance, you may need supply warehouses or repair and replacement centers in several locations.

Of course, when you need more space, you once again have to choose the best locations. This time it will be both easier and more difficult. It's easier because you have a better idea what you're looking for. It's more difficult because you have a more exact idea what you need. That is, since you understand your requirements better this time around, you'll be both more confident and more particular about your choices.

FACE UP TO COMPETITION

When you're scouting expansion locations, be very aware of competition in your new areas. While you managed one small business in one location, you probably didn't attract much notice from larger companies. However, once you start expanding, you're apt to attract attention.

Large corporations are in business for the same basic reason you are: to make money. The sheer size of a big company means it has to make large amounts of money just to support itself. At the same time, most good-sized businesses have stockholders to answer to.

These investors expect maximum returns on their money. When they don't get them, they can become very unpleasant. Failure to pay dividends to the stockholders very often leads to unemployment for a company's top executives. Therefore, corporate executives are very sensitive to any threat to their market position. If they think you might siphon away some of their customers, and thereby some of their income, they can play rough.

A common tactic large businesses use to get rid of competition is the price war. Many small business owners are driven under when one branch of a large chain undersells them for months on end. Once the small business closes, the chain's branch raises prices. This works because other branches of the chain support the branch that drops prices. The small business doesn't have multiple sources of income, and can't cut prices and stay in business long enough to outlast the chain.

Occasionally large businesses go in for industrial spying or sabotage. This may take the form of paying someone in your company to reveal your plans and ideas. Then the large competitor, with the advantage of greater resources, can introduce your plans sooner than you do, over a wider area. Once in a while, too, you hear of actual criminal acts directed against a business. While this is rare, it does happen, and you should be alert to it.

The smaller business does have some advantages in these competitions. One is that your smaller size makes it easier to keep track of your employees and what they're doing. You can get to know them personally, and inspire their loyalty to you.

Another is that you can specialize in small market niches that are simply not profitable enough for a large corporation to be interested. Sometimes large companies are even glad when a small competitor takes over some function the big company had to provide because customers needed it, but which didn't really suit the needs of the corporation.

Your real strong point, though, is in quality and customer relations. It's easier to control quality when you run a smaller operation. It's also much easier to treat customers as individuals and see that they get prompt, courteous service.

Many, many people are disgusted with big companies. Unhappy customers complain about being treated like faceless robots whose main function is to hand over their incomes to the corporations. This was the corporate attitude that led to AT&T being broken up by the government. Remember comedienne Lily Tomlin as Ernestine, the arrogant telephone operator? She became famous with such lines as "We don't have to be nice, we're the phone company."

We all laughed, but we also saw the truth behind the comedy. Big companies lose good will when they don't concern themselves with the customer's needs. Years later the phone company learned this, when customers were allowed to sign up for alternate services like Sprint and MCI. Now the phone company wants to be nice, but it's too late.

In a small business, you have much greater opportunity to treat each and every customer with respect and friendship. Make sure everyone who works for you gets the message. Don't allow customers to be treated as though they only annoy you and interrupt your employees' personal conversations. They're paying your overhead, supporting your families, and putting your children through college. Since they do so much for you, make sure they get the best from you.

Another way you can protect yourself against competition from larger companies is to make sure they don't move in too close to you. I heard last year about a family of Vietnamese refugees who opened a small liquor and convenience store in a neighborhood shopping strip. They asked for and got a clause in their lease that said the owner of the shopping strip wouldn't rent space to any other liquor outlet. If the owner breached that clause, he had to pay compensation.

A strange thing happened in that case. The strip owner got a very good offer from a large chain of discount liquor stores to rent a vacancy in the strip. The owner decided the profit from that lease would be worth it, but he asked the discount chain to pay the compensation to the small store.

The Vietnamese got a nice chunk of cash, and continued to run their little store. Eighteen months later, the large chain went out of business. The little store is still there, and the refugees got to keep the nice cash bonus their former competitor paid them. There's a family that agrees with me that the United States of America is the best country in the world for the independent entrepreneur.

You can't always count on such a perfect solution to competitive pressures. You must be prepared for them, though. When you know the competition and the possible forms it may take, you can prepare to meet it and beat it.

TAKE STOCK OF
YOUR PEOPLE

When you're this far along with growth plans — knowing your potential market, your physical needs, and the new locations you want — it's time to look at your staff requirements.

First, consider the people who already work for you. Are some of them capable of taking on more responsibility? For example, can your personal assistant or your production manager take on running an entire new branch alone? Which departments have to grow? How many people will they need, with what skills? Do the people now in charge of these departments have the ability to run a larger operation, or should you put someone else in charge? Can some of these people be retrained or educated to better positions?

By and large, transitions go more smoothly when you promote from within your company wherever possible. Bringing in someone new to take over causes friction between the newcomer and the old hands. This is particularly true when one of the old hands was in charge of a department and you put a stranger over him or her.

Sometimes, though, one or more of your original staff just isn't capable of handling increased responsibility or authority. Occasionally these people even realize it themselves. It's only fair to talk to them about it in advance. Explain what the expanded position will entail, and your concerns about the type of person needed in that job.

If the person feels capable of more growth, you may decide to allow it, but keep a very close eye on him or her. Be ready to guide and advise often, and keep in mind you still may have to make a replacement.

When it's obvious someone can't handle new duties, decide why. It's always possible the job has simply grown too large for anyone to function well in it. You may have to break the job, or even the entire department, into two or more separate components.

The answer, however, may be that your old employee isn't up to the demands caused by your company's growth. In that case, you can't afford to let sentiment override your judgment. Explain, as tactfully and truthfully as you can, that you must hire someone with more experience.

Allow your employee a choice of leaving the company or taking a subordinate position. Don't demand a decision immediately, but encourage the person to think it over for a few days, discuss it with a spouse, and maybe even meet the replacement first.

Some people will elect to leave immediately, while others will adopt a wait-and-see attitude. You can expect, though, that about half of these will leave within a short time. If you don't want that to happen because the person has a particular expertise you value, consider creating a new position and asking the person to fill it, rather than replacing or demoting him or her.

All these staffing considerations involve money. When you increase the number of people you employ, you increase your payroll. When you ask people to take on more work, they expect to be paid more. If you can afford it, of course they should be given raises immediately. However, your business might also lend itself to profit sharing or bonuses based on how well the new venture does.

Information on all these new plans will give you a basis to make overhead and profit projections for your expansion. (Don't forget to include the cost of new business licenses, incorporation, or other government registrations.) At this point, you may find you need more money than you thought.

WHEN COSTS
EXCEED CREDIT

As I mentioned earlier in this chapter, you should have already made sure you have a good line of credit available. If this won't be enough, though, go after other forms of financing. You proceed with this just as you would for start-up funds.

Prepare a careful business plan, including all the research you've done on the potential market, locations and their prices, advertising plans, staff needs, and all the other considerations we've just covered. Then present your plan to potential lenders, including possible partners, banks, and venture capitalists.

This is a point when, if you haven't already done so, you should consider incorporating. Talk to your attorney about the possibilities for issuing stock or attracting private investors. And good luck in your future growth.

Whether you choose to expand to the limits of your industry or stay small, there's one point all entrepreneurs consider at some time. That's what to do about retirement. (Some days we think more seriously about it than others.)

There are several different ways to handle retirement, and some advance planning to do for each of them. Therefore, I'd like to finish this book with a chapter on ways to end your business involvement.

CHAPTER 12

REAPING YOUR REWARD

Eventually you'll retire from the business you built from nothing. You don't simply wake up one day, decide "This is it!" and never go in to work again, though. You make plans ahead of time, choosing the method that's best for you, your company, and your successors, if any.

Of course, if you have a very individualized enterprise, leaving it may be almost as simple as deciding you're through working. Those who write, act, or paint pictures for a living can't very well hand over their businesses to someone else.

You can, however, make arrangements for any unsold inventory you have on hand. People in creative arts should choose reputable agents to administer their remaining rights and income. They also need wills which spell out the disposition of rights to their work and income from it after their deaths.

In addition, any regular employees should be notified well in advance of the artist's coming retirement. Those who may no longer be needed, such as a secretary, should be given a good recommendation and perhaps a parting bonus.

If you've built the kind of enterprise that can be taken over by someone else, you have many more choices open to you. You might pass the business along to a relative; lease the rights to your name or products; sell part of it, keeping an interest for yourself; sell it with a provision that you're retained as a consultant or director; sell all your interests; or liquidate completely.

The first question you have to answer, of course, is which of these methods will work for your company. Do you have any relatives with the interest and ability to step into your shoes? Does the business have a name or product someone would care to lease? Would the company be attractive to a potential buyer? Are there assets that would bring a good price in a liquidation sale?

GROOMING YOUR HEIR

If you have an heir who shows promise, you should of course start training that person to take over as early as possible. Some young people scoff at the idea of starting "from the ground up," but it's not such a bad way to learn. As I keep stressing, the owner of a business needs insight into every job, every department.

When you build the company yourself, you learn what you need as you go along. But those who come in at the executive level without ever learning what happens in the stock room or on the assembly line don't have that advantage. I think that's one of the main problems large companies face in this country today. Too many business leaders got all their learning from college textbooks, and don't have practical experience in the day-to-day work of their companies.

Naturally, your heir won't get exactly the same training you did. There isn't the make-or-break pressure to succeed when the business is already profitable. But learning what goes on, coupled with your advice and a good business education, will put any young person way out in front when he or she takes over.

WHAT'S BEST FOR YOU?

What you want for yourself in retirement is just as important as the possibilities available for selling. Some people, when they're ready to retire, want nothing to do with their former business. They want to walk away and never think about it again.

Others like the idea of "keeping a hand in." They depend on retaining a share of the business to assure their retirement income. At the same time, they want to know the company's run right so their income continues and increases.

Finally, is the business worth more with or without your input? A few businesses are so unique, only the original owner can show someone else how to run it. Occasionally, too, you'll find an interested buyer who has good business sense and the desire to learn, but not much experience. This potential buyer may pay top dollar if you spend one to three years teaching him or her the ropes.

The reverse of this is the business that needs some fresh ideas to remain profitable. Like it or not, some of us do get a little rusty in our thinking. We keep doing what worked in the past instead of changing with the times. In these cases, a new owner may prefer a free hand to innovate. If you hang on to enough authority to block new ideas, you may find no one wants your business even at a reduced price.

GETTING THE
RIGHT PRICE

Whatever your decision, when the time comes to leave, you want a fair return for the interests you sell. Your accountant or a business broker can help you with an appraisal.

The price of a business depends on many different factors. Cash flow and volume of business, customer lists, leases, desirable locations, machinery, office equipment, accounts payable and receivable, and all other assets and liabilities have to be figured in. Then a sum can be added for intangibles such as good will or future prospects.

For example, if you own a buggy whip company, chances are business won't pick up much in the future. But if you market computer software that's the hottest thing since IBM saw its first chip, your potential is valuable.

Some entrepreneurs get into the habit of hiding information. They keep more than one set of books, carry several bank accounts, and borrow and run lines of credit through numerous lenders. When it comes time to sell, this can get you into trouble.

In the first place, hiding assets reduces the value of the business, and the eventual price someone will pay for it. In the second place, keeping debts and liabilities from someone who's about to become responsible for them is fraud.

Anyone intelligent enough to run your business should make a complete credit check on both you and the company before making an offer. And certainly any buyer will do a complete audit within a few months of taking over the business. It may take time, but any tangle of complicated bookkeeping you've created to hide the facts will be unwound. If you've withheld important information, or represented your business as more profitable than it actually is, you can be prosecuted. Keep your books honestly and give your buyer a true accounting to avoid legal action.

What do you do if you get your appraisal and find the price isn't high enough to buy you the retirement you want? You have a couple of alternatives. You can sell anyway, and invest the money in something else. Or sell off only part of the business and become a silent partner.

To avoid this possibility, have your business appraised every so often over the years. Know what it's worth, not just on paper, but on the open market. This gives you time to make plans. You could then expand more than you originally intended. Or you could sell and start something you think will be more profitable. Or you could buy several partnerships in other businesses, and let other people build your retirement fund for you. This is another area where your accountant's advice will help.

When you sell a business, financing can take several different forms. Most common, though, is to let the business buy you out. The new owner pays you an initial down payment of anywhere from five to twenty percent of the full price. The balance, plus interest, is paid over a period of years out of profits, either as a fixed sum or as a percentage of either net or gross.

As the seller, you want to get the maximum amount possible without endangering the business. After all, if it loses money, you may never be paid. Therefore, think long and carefully before you agree to any creative terms. It's always a temptation to ask for a large chunk of the gross, but this could hamper future prosperity. It's better for both of you if you settle for a percentage of the net, but specify a minimum sum.

When you include your services as advisor, teacher, or consultant, you of course get a higher price. This could be in the form of more money for the sale. It could also be designated as a salary or fee in addition to the sale price.

The length of the buyout period could be three years, or twenty, or anything in between. Before negotiating this, be sure to look at how it will affect your tax position.

FINDING THE MARKET

When you're ready to sell, there are several ways to locate potential buyers. The simplest, of course, is to list it in classified ads. Newspapers, business opportunity papers and magazines, and trade journals are good places to advertise.

You can also list with business brokers. These are agents, like real estate agents, who specialize in arranging sales and purchases of companies. They charge a fairly high commission, up to ten percent of the final purchase price. As with any other type of agent, there are good ones and bad ones. Talk with other business owners, especially those who have recently bought or sold a company, for recommendations.

One of the most often overlooked yet most likely sources of purchasers is among your competition. Buying you out serves a dual purpose for them. They eliminate future competition from your company under new ownership; at the same time they expand their own operation without going through many of the steps we discussed in the previous chapter. They take over proven locations, trained staff, valuable customer lists, inventory, and equipment. Your business is probably worth more to a competitor than to any other possible purchaser.

Another good place to look is among your own employees, particularly your executive staff. They know the business better than any outsider, and have been trained by you in how to run it. Furthermore, if you sell to someone else, your old staff may lose their jobs.

Frequently, too, lower-level workers want the chance to share ownership in the company they work for. There have been several cases in the last few years of everyone in a company chipping in to buy it and keep it running. Usually in the past these have been situations where the owners were planning to close down the business, and the workers acted to save their jobs. However, I see no reason why it wouldn't work just as well for a going concern.

EMPLOYEES IN TRANSITION

This is a solution to one of the larger problems employees face when they learn the company they work for is about to be sold. You may think it won't affect you, since you're leaving anyway. But you're likely to feel the repercussions of employee concerns long before the papers are signed, and it could even lower your sale price.

You see, as soon as your workers learn the company is up for sale, they start worrying. (And they will learn about it.) They'll worry about whether the new owner will replace everybody; whether working hours or conditions will change; if they'll keep their benefits and seniority; if the new boss will bring in his or her own management team and supervisors and put them over all the people who have authority now; if they'll lose their parking space, corner office, personal secretary, company car, overtime pay, company bowling league, or whatever else they have.

Rumors will travel around your company faster than the speed of light. If you could hear them all, you'd be astonished at the inventiveness they show. You might even think that if all these people applied half that imagination to their jobs, the company would be worth ten times as much.

This is human nature. When people don't know what's going on, they gossip, speculate, and listen to wild ideas. It would be funny, if the potential results weren't so bad.

One possibility is that people spend so much time gossiping and worrying that their job performance suffers. This lowers productivity — and profits — right when you want them at their best.

Some people may quit. They become so afraid of the unknown that they act to relieve their own anxieties. This leaves you with a hiring and training problem, which again reduces productivity. And when the rumors have reached outside the company, it can be harder to find replacements for the people who left.

Who wants to take a job with an outfit being bought by a group of Arabs who intend to move the entire operation to the Saudi desert? Or an Oriental group planning to introduce twelve-hour days, compulsory calisthenics, and meditation breaks, and to replace the company health plan with acupuncture and herbal teas?

I'm not kidding. These rumors, and even wilder ones, get started all the time. The worst one I ever heard was the financial services business that was supposedly being bought by a religious cult. Everyone was going to be required to convert, shave their heads, wear long robes, and devote one day a week to begging in the city park. People from the mail room right up to vice presidents had heard that one, and many of them believed it.

The best thing you can do about this problem — in fact, the only thing — is be truthful with your employees. When you have offers for the company, tell your staff who made the offer, and how seriously you're considering it. If your company is very large, you may only need to tell the executive staff, but be sure at least they know what's going on.

Try, as well as you can, to safeguard your employees' interests. After all, they've put their time and work into your business and helped you build whatever value it has now. If possible, negotiate a sale that gives your people some protection.

You can't tie the hands of a new owner for long, of course. No one will buy a business when they have to run it indefinitely the same way, and with the same people, as the previous owner did. You wouldn't want someone else telling you how to run your own company. After all, isn't independence at least part of the reason you went into business for yourself in the first place?

You can ask, however, for some sort of guarantee. You might ask for executives to be granted either a full year of employment after the sale or severance pay equal to salary and benefits for whatever remains of the year when they're dismissed. Lower level positions might be compensated in descending amounts of employment length and/or severance pay.

Just because you ask, of course, doesn't mean you'll get everything you want. Both you and your employees have to accept that life is full of changes. When the business is sold, everyone must adjust to the new owner's management.

It will help all of you through the transition, though, if your people know you're thinking of them. It may even keep your key people around long enough to find out if they can work with the new boss or not. And that's about the best you can do for them.

PREPARE
YOURSELF

What's the best you can do for yourself? About anything you want, at this point. Just be sure you do have something you want.

I'm always amazed at stories I hear of people who retire without the slightest idea what they'll do with the rest of their lives. You've probably heard the same kinds of tales. "Poor old Jake. He worked so hard building that company up from nothing. Then he sold it, retired, and was dead in six months."

Or how about this one? "Too bad about Maddie. She used to be so sharp. Put her husband through college, raised four kids, then went back to school herself, and started a business when she was in her forties. Now she can finally relax and enjoy life, but all she does is stare out the window. She didn't even recognize her daughter when she came to visit."

It's no joke. Doctors and psychologists tell us we all need a reason to keep living, something to look forward to. Science is just beginning to learn why so many otherwise healthy people die or become senile shortly after retiring. They just plain lose interest in the world around them.

That's a terrible waste. Don't let it happen to you. Unfortunately, I think entrepreneurs are more prone to this sort of thing than a lot of other groups. We're used to exciting, challenging lives. We spend a lot of time working for our successes — maybe, sometimes, a little too much time.

Then, when our chance to enjoy everything we worked for finally comes, we don't know how to do it. We aren't used to facing unscheduled days with no meetings, decisions, crises, or triumphs. Life seems dull without the work we're so used to.

Plan now for the day when you retire. Make lists of things you'd like to do when you have the time — books to read, hobbies to take up, courses to study, countries to visit — whatever sounds interesting to you.

Collect names and addresses of groups involved in fun or worthwhile activities you're interested in, but don't have time for

---

right now. Antique car collectors, charities, the Peace Corps, or a bridge club; this country is brimming with opportunities to add enjoyment to your life or contribute to someone else's.

If you have a chance, check out some of these ideas in advance to find out which ones interest you most. Then, a year or more before you actually retire, start pursuing a couple of them. Learn the special terms, the language; get to know some other people involved.

Of course, you can't sail around the world on a yacht, or start running an Australian sheep ranch, while you're still tied to most businesses. But you can read up on the subject, collect brochures, attend meetings or lectures. Give yourself some background, just as you did in starting your business.

GOALS ARE
STILL IMPORTANT

Once you're retired, set goals for yourself: I'll get my golf handicap down to fifteen by next July; sign up for the square dance class in September; find a blind child to read to in May; learn three new bird species a week; call a photographer tomorrow and get a set of pictures made to send around to modeling agencies; etc. Write your goals down, talk them up, commit yourself so you can't back out. Make phone calls and appointments. Meet people and make friends among those who share your interests.

You may feel a little lost at first. Remember, it's all part of starting something new. You felt the same way the first time your mother dropped you off at kindergarten, the day you entered high school, the first day on your first job, the first time you went out alone on a date, the day you opened your business, and several times after that. It's part of life, and as long as you can still feel that way, you're still alive.

Have a little patience, and pretty soon you'll forget all about that feeling of strangeness. You'll be caught up in an entirely new phase of your life, one with its own challenges and rewards. And you'll be equipped to enjoy it completely, because you've already earned the most important part — your independence.

CONCLUSION

T here you have it: my outline for how to start and build your own business, whatever it may be. I hope you use this book as the starting point for the success you want and deserve.
Remember, though, as I told you before, this is only the beginning. It's up to you to take it from here. You'll have to make choices, set goals, and find answers for yourself. No one else can do it for you, because no one else knows exactly what you want and need.

You know, though. You know what's best for you, what you're capable of, and how far you want to go. That's why you have to be the key to your own success; no one else's blueprint can ever be right for the individual you are.

That's why it's so important to establish your own goals. Without goals, something to steer for, too many people drift through their lives and end up nowhere. I believe each and every one of us has the potential to make our own choices, set our own courses, and reach

---

the goals we set for ourselves — if we really want to.

It doesn't happen in a day, or a month, or a year. We have to work steadily for what we want, a little bit at a time. That means planning ahead, and then having the discipline to stay with the plan. Yes, it's the formula I use in my lectures and other books. System + Discipline = Success.

The reason I repeat this so often is, I know it works. It works for me, and it works for thousands of my students all over the country. When you study the lives of people who succeed in every age, in every walk of life, you find the same pattern. They established a system to follow, and then had the discipline to follow through until they reached their goals.

I want everyone to reach their goals, just as I've reached so many of mine, and know the rewards of well-earned happiness and prosperity. When you have questions, and you will, you'll find the answers exist. All you have to do is look for them.

Finally, my last words to you are: Believe in yourself. You have within you all the potential you need to do whatever you truly want to, as long as you're willing to try and keep trying. The only failure is failing to try; so when problems come up and you suffer setbacks, don't lose faith. We learn from everything we experience, so believe in your success and keep working for it.

RECOMMENDED READING

T hese are a few of the books I've found helpful over the years, plus a couple I've included especially for women. You'll find your own favorites as you do your own study and research, but this is a helpful list if you don't know where to start. Some of these books are practical, some are inspirational, but all of them have something valuable to say to the entrepreneur. If you're interested in one but can't find a copy in your local library, ask a bookstore to order it for you.

A Whack on the Side of the Head, Roger von Oech, Ph.D. Warner Books, 1983.

Coaching for Improved Work Performance, Ferdinand F. Fournies. Van Nostrand Reinhold Company, 1978.

Doing It Now, Edwin C. Bliss. Charles Scribner's Sons, 1983.

The Effective Executive, Peter F. Drucker. Harper andRow, 1966, 1967.

Executive Policy and Strategic Planning, Thomas J. McNichols. McGraw-Hill Book Company, 1977.

How Managers Motivate, William F. Dowling and Leonard R. Sayles. McGraw-Hill Book Company, 1978.

How To Be Your Own Management Consultant, Kenneth J. Albert. McGraw-Hill Book Company, 1978.

How To Make Meetings Work, Michael Doyle and David Straus. Wyden Books, 1976.

How To Run Any Organization, Theodore Caplow. Holt, Rinehart and Winston, 1976.

Management: Tasks, Responsibilities, Practices, Peter F. Drucker. Harper and Row, 1973, 1974.

The Managerial Woman, Margaret Henning and Anne Jardim. Anchor Press/Doubleday, 1977.

Megatrends, John Naisbitt. Warner Books, 1982.

Moneylove, Jerry Gillies. Warner Books, 1978.

1001 Ways To Be Your Own Boss, Vivo Bennett and Cricket Clagett. Prentice-Hall, Inc., 1976.

Overcoming the Fear of Success, Martha Friedman. Warner Books, 1980.

Procrastination: Why You Do It, What To Do About It, Jane B. Burka, Ph.D., and Lenora M. Yuen, Ph.D. Addison-Wesley Publishing Company, 1983.

Success Is Not and Accident, John G. Kappas, Ph.D. Panorama Publishing Company, 1982.

Women, Money, & Power, Phyllis Chesler and Emily Jane Goodman. William Morrow and Company, Inc., 1976.